BELIEVING
and LIVING

A text for the WJEC GCSE Short Course

by **Gavin Craigen** and **Joy White**

WJEC
CBAC

Hodder & Stoughton
A MEMBER OF THE HODDER HEADLINE GROUP

Joy and Gavin would like to thank the following for their help and contributions: Rachel O'Connor and Valerie Bingham of Hodder & Stoughton - for commencing the project and helping to see it through all the snags and difficulties, being so understanding, and never giving up hope; Tudor Thomas of WJEC - for his constant encouragement and support, and Roger Owen - for his helpful comments and advice; Daniel Crabbe (Graphics Artist) - for his superb interpretation of ideas; and most of all Brendan Schmack and Fiona Craigen - for their constant care, support and patience throughout the period of working towards publication.

The publishers would like to thank the following for permission to reproduce material in this book:

'Who Made A Mess?' p16, taken from *The Day I Fell Down The Toilet* by Steve Turner published by Lion Publishing and reproduced by permission; 'Prayer for Agunot' International Coalition for Agunah Rights; p45, Belief in God graph p72, reproduced by permission, *The Tablet*, the international catholic weekly; 'Guardian Angel' p74, from *A Hand on My Shoulder* by N. Cook and V. Frampton, New Cherwell Press, Oxford; 'Mother to die after 21 years in coma' p80, *The Evening Standard*.

The publishers would like to thank the following individuals, institutions and companies for permission to reproduce photographs and illustrations in this book:

Life File/Emma Lee pp2 t/l; t/c/r; c/l; btm l & c; 3, 4; Oxford Scientific Films/Breck P Kent p2 t/c/l; Science Photo Library/Charles D.Winters p2 b/r; Science Photo Library/Astrid & Hanns-Frieder Michler p2 c/r; Science Photo Library/Russ Lappa p2 t/r; NASA p7; Corbis pp8, 32l, 73bl, 75b, 76tl, 97, 101; Science Photo Library/John Sanford p11; Science Photo Library/Claude Nuridsany & Marie Perennou p12; Revd Dr John Polkinghorne p13; Christian Aid and CAFOD p16; Popperfoto/Guillerno Granja p17; Ann & Bury Peerless pp22t, 76br; News Team International p22b; John Rifkin pp23, 45; Twin Studios/CIRCA Photo Library Life File/Nicola Sutton p29l & r; Format/Jacky Chapman pp29cl, 46, 77c; Telegraph Colour Library p29cr; True Love Waits p32; Popperfoto/Jonathan Evans p 38; Corbis/Liba Taylor p 49l; CIRCA/Mike Edwards p 49c; Life File/Louise Oldroyd pp49, 78t; CIRCA/Bipin J. Mistry p50; Peter Sanders pp51l, 69b, 70l, 76bl, 87, 109tl; CIRCA/John Smith pp51r, 67, 69t, 75tr, 75ct, 99, 109; CIRCA/Barrie Searle pp52l, 70r; Corbis/David Reed p52r; Corbis/Enzo & Paolo Ragazzini p73tl; The Salvation Army pp73tl, 94; CIRCA/William Holtby pp73cl, 76c; Topham/Press Association/Fiona Hanson p73c; Popperfoto/Fred Prouser p73cl; Life File/Richard Powers p75tl; Corbis/Dave Bartruff p75cb; CIRCA/Ged Murray p76tl; Christine Osborne Pictures pp77tl, 109bl & br; Tzedek UK pp77tr, 103, (Steve Derby/Tzedek) 103tr, 115; ISKON Educational Services pp77b, 92cl, 98; Life File/John Dakers p78b; The Samaritans p81; Corbis/David & Peter Turnley p83; AKG London/'The Ascent to the Heavenly Paradise' by Hieronymus Bosch p85; Impact Visuals/Donna Binder p92tl; Catholic Association for Racial Justice pp92tc, 96; The Press Association Ltd 2001 p92tr; Christian Aid/Brenda Hayward p92cr; Format/Pam Isherwood p92bl; Drop the Debt p92br; Gavin Craigen p95; Illustrated London News p97tl; The Muslim Women's Helpline p100; Christian Aid p104; CAFOD p104; Tearfund p104; Format/Melanie Friend p106; Show Racism the Red Card p108; Popperfoto/Reinhard Krause p110; The Message Trust p112; Muslim Aid p114.

(t top; c centre; b bottom; l left; r right)

Every effort has been made to contact the holders of copyright material but if any have been inadvertently overlooked, the publishers will be pleased to make the necessary alterations at the first opportunity.

Orders: please contact Bookpoint Ltd, 130 Milton Park, Abingdon, Oxon OX14 4SB.
Telephone (44) 01235 827720, Fax (44) 01235 400454. Lines are open from 9.00–6.00, Monday to Saturday, with a 24 hour message answering service. Email address: orders@bookpoint.co.uk

British Library Cataloguing in Publication Data

A catalogue record for this title is available from The British Library

ISBN 0 340 80215 4

First published 2001
Impression number 10 9 8 7 6 5 4 3 2
Year   2006 2005 2004 2003 2002

Copyright © 2001 Gavin Craigen and Joy White

Cover photos (l to r) from Corbis/Photodisc/Photodisc/Flip Schulke: Corbis/Corbis
Designed by Pentacor plc, High Wycombe
Printed in Italy for Hodder & Stoughton Educational,
a division of Hodder Headline Plc, 338 Euston Road, London NW1 3BH.

Contents

Our world

(If you are doing the Internal Assessment option,
the content of this chapter will be the focus for your work.)

What makes us human?

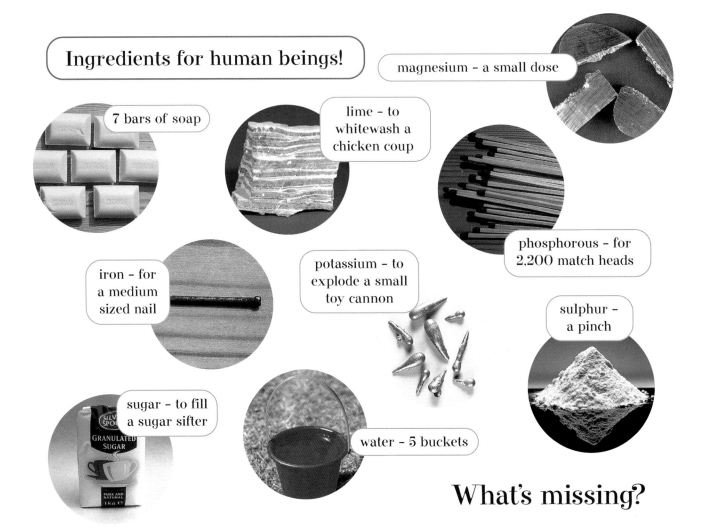

Ingredients for human beings!

magnesium – a small dose

7 bars of soap

lime – to whitewash a chicken coup

phosphorous – for 2,200 match heads

iron – for a medium sized nail

potassium – to explode a small toy cannon

sulphur – a pinch

sugar – to fill a sugar sifter

water – 5 buckets

What's missing?

When we start asking questions about ourselves, we find there are many different aspects that make us the people we are.

We have **bodies** that grow and help us live and move;

We have **minds** to think and decide;

We have **personalities** that make us different from other people;

We have **emotions** through which we react;

We also have **experiences** and **influences** that affect the kind of people we are and the decisions we make.

parents · family · other adults · friends · grandparents · teachers · acquaintances · school · books · community · television · culture · advertising · laws · music · religion · fashion · country · magazines · newspapers

Task

- What are your major influences?
- Rank order these influences for your life.

Exam Tip

When giving more than one example, make sure you give different examples. Many candidates lose marks because they repeat the same answer using different words.

Q State **two** influences on people, that affect their character, attitude and values. [2]

Look at the two answers below. Which do you think is better, and why?

Answer A	Answer B
(i) Religion	(i) religious beliefs
(ii) Beliefs	(ii) personal background or upbringing

Answer A was awarded 1 mark and Answer B, 2 marks.

Can you explain why?

Can you think of other possible answers?

Try and group them so that you are sure which are different words to describe the same thing.

Why are we here?

> To try and make the world a better place.

> People do not live nowadays; they get about 10% out of life.

> ❝ You have made us to know you, God, and we die restless until we know you. ❞
>
> (St Augustine)

> Someday I want to be rich

> To do all the things I want to do and go all the places I want to go to.

People give many different reasons why they exist, but many people, whether they are religious or not, think that it is important for humanity to care for each other and for the planet.

All religions teach that human beings are unique and different from all other animals.

Check it out

Humanity

Compassion for others

Benevolence

Caring about other human beings

Kind heartedness to others

INTELLIGENCE	the ability to think and reflect; to apply knowledge and learning; to reason
MORALITY	a sense of right and wrong; values
LANGUAGE	the ability to write/read languages; use of learned languages

Christians would add that another important difference is **REVELATION**. By this they mean that humanity is:

> *Created in God's image; capable of religious behaviour and beliefs; having a conscience; in possession of a 'soul'*

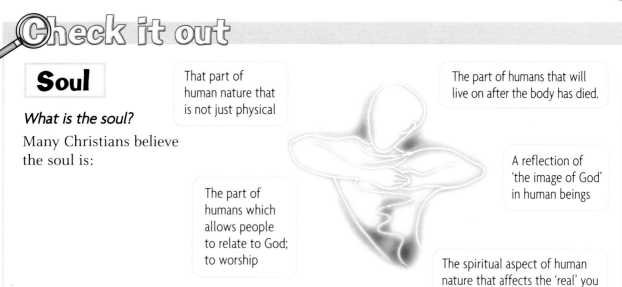

Check it out

Soul

What is the soul?

Many Christians believe the soul is:

That part of human nature that is not just physical

The part of humans that will live on after the body has died.

The part of humans which allows people to relate to God; to worship

A reflection of 'the image of God' in human beings

The spiritual aspect of human nature that affects the 'real' you

Throughout many religious and sacred books we read how humanity has a number of purposes and responsibilities in life.

Christianity	
Genesis 1: 16	To enjoy the garden/world and its fruits/resources *['You are free to eat from any tree in the garden']*
Genesis 1: 17	To obey God *['You must not eat of the tree of knowledge of good and evil']*
Genesis 1: 26	**Stewardship** of the earth (to look after it for God) *['Let them have dominion over the fish of the sea …']*
Genesis 1: 28	To have sexual relationships and children *['Be fruitful and multiply, and fill the earth']*
Mark 12: 30	To serve God and live for him (this includes telling others about and sharing one's faith) *['Love God with all your heart, mind, soul and strength']*
Mark 12: 31	To live in harmony with others *['Love your neighbour as yourself']*

Judaism	
Genesis 1: 16	To enjoy the garden/world and its fruits/resources *['You are free to eat from any tree in the garden']*
Genesis 1: 17	To obey God *['You must not eat of the tree of knowledge of good and evil']*
Genesis 1: 26	**Stewardship** of the earth (to look after it for God) *['Let them have dominion over the fish of the sea …']*
Genesis 1: 28	To have sexual relationships and children *['Be fruitful and multiply, and fill the earth']*
Deuteronomy 20: 19	To preserve trees in times of war *['You shall not destroy its trees by wielding an axe against them']*
Leviticus 19: 18	To live in harmony with others *['You shall love your neighbour as yourself']*

Islam	
Surah 6: 165	To act as **khalifahs**, or guardians of the planet *['He has made you His ruling agents in the earth']*

 **Exam Tip**

Quoting the Texts

ALWAYS *use* any quotations from sacred texts to support or illustrate your answer;

NEVER just quote or copy texts as an answer.

 Q *Describe the teachings about looking after the world in one religious tradition.* [6]

Look at the two answers below, and using the Levels of Response Grids on page 117, decide what marks you would give to Answer A and Answer B, and why?

Answer A	Answer B
Name of religious tradition: Islam	Name of religious tradition: Christianity
Teaching about looking after the world: Muslims believe that Allah made the world and everything that is in it. Humans are seen as the most important, and are understood to be khalifahs, or trustees, as it says in Surah 6:165 'He has made you His ruling agents in the earth'. It is therefore humanity's responsibility to maintain the pattern and balance (or fitrah) in the world. To do this requires humans to actively use their skills to look after the environment and not allow it to be spoiled. Islam regards this as very important, and humans will be questioned about their 'caretaking' for Allah on the Day of Judgement.	Teaching about looking after the world: Christians believe 'And God said to them, Be fruitful and multiply, and fill the earth and subdue it; and have dominion over the fish of the sea and over the birds of the air, and also over every living thing that moves upon the earth.' (Genesis 1: 28) They also believe 'The Lord God took the man and put him in the Garden of Eden to till it and keep it.' (Genesis 2: 15)

How did our universe begin?

Almost throughout human history, people have asked this question.

To many religious people there is little doubt that God is the cause or creator of the universe.

As humans have discovered more and more about the universe, so scientists began to construct theories about its beginnings. To some people it seemed that such ideas replaced the beliefs in God as the originator of all things.

There are many different views as to how the universe began. Within Christianity, Hinduism, Islam and Judaism, we find stories of creation which are often interpreted in different ways.

the 1st day

the 6th day

the 2nd day

the 7th day -holy

the 5th day

the 3rd day

the 4th day

Check it out

Creation

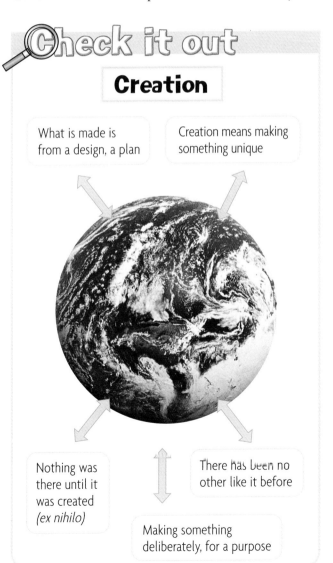

What is made is from a design, a plan

Creation means making something unique

Nothing was there until it was created (ex nihilo)

There has been no other like it before

Making something deliberately, for a purpose

Creation in Judaism and Christianity

Jews and Christians share the same story of Creation, found in Genesis 1 and 2. In this story it makes clear the belief that God created everything that is in the heavens and the earth:

- Light and dark
- Sun, moon and stars
- Day and night
- All kinds of living creatures
- Time and seasons
- Human beings
- Land, sea and sky.

> ❛And God looked at all that He had created, and behold, it was good.❜
>
> (Genesis 1: 31)

All these were created in 'six days', and on the seventh day God rested.

There are different responses to this story within Christianity and Judaism.

'The earth belongs to God!
Everything in all the world is his!
He is the one who pushed oceans
back to let dry land appear.'

(Psalm 24: 1–2)

'I am a practising Christian but do not believe every detail of the creation happened like it says in Genesis. The importance of the story is not how God created the earth, but that he did!'

Helen, age 16

'As a Christian I believe every word in the Bible is true. Yes it's an amazing story about the creation — but God is amazing!'

Mark, age 18

Literalist views e.g. Mark	Non-literalist views e.g. Helen	
The main points of the story actually happened the way they are described – literally: ● God's spirit moved across the waters ● There were six days of 24 hours in which God created ● Adam was formed out of the dust of the earth ● Eve was formed out of Adam's rib. *Believers of this view see a conflict between science and religion, and are convinced of the truth of the Bible in a literal and fundamental sense.*	The main point of the story is not to detail **how** God created, but to state that he did. So the story is not a literal account, but does contain important truths – such as: ● God did create the world ● That he used the natural processes he created ● That there were clear 'periods' of creation, though not 24 hours as such. *People who accept this view, see no real conflict between scientific theories and religion, and can see how both weave together to give a full picture of life and the earth.*	The story is entirely poetic and/or mythical. It is not true, and contains no literal truth, but is describing what the writers of the time believed to be true. Scientific knowledge and discovery have shown the ideas of creation to be unacceptable. *People who think this believe that scientific explanations, based on evidence and research, are irrefutable, and that religious ideas are a different (and less trustworthy) kind of statement.*

Whatever position a person takes, it would seem true to say that, in general, Christians and Jews would agree that the Genesis story illustrates some important key beliefs:

- *God created everything for a purpose*
- *The beginning of the world and of life was not accidental*
- *Human beings are different from other creatured, in being in the 'image of God', and sharing some responsibility for the world*
- *That the world created was basically good.*

❝The stories of creation ... are not intended to teach scientific truths, as we would understand them today. They are actually intended to teach religious truths. For example, they teach us that the universe was created by God, that it didn't just come into existence on its own, and that the universe as a whole is good.❞

(Professor Nancy Murphy, speaking on *The Question Is...?* video)

- Here is an answer that gets 2 marks. What would you add to give it a Level 3 and 6 marks? (see page 117)

Q *Describe the beliefs from one religious tradition about the world and the purpose of human beings.* [6]

Name of religious tradition: Judaism

Beliefs about the world and the purpose of human beings: Jews believe God created the earth and that humans were given the job of being stewards for God. They also believe it is each person's responsibility to do mitzvot, or good deeds, in the world. Jews also have rules about the environment – food laws and things like that.

Creation in Islam

- Allah made the heaven and earth, and all the animals, birds and fish; the sun, moon and stars; the plants and rain; and the angels
- The angels were sent to bring seven handfuls of earth – each of a different colour
- From these the first man, Adam, was made; and from his side, Eve – the first woman
- They lived in Paradise – a beautiful garden; where they could eat anything, except the fruit of one tree
- On disobeying Allah, after being tempted by Iblis they were placed outside the garden as a punishment.

He has made you His ruling agents in the earth, and has given some of you higher rank than others, so that He might test you in the gifts He has given you. Your Lord is quick to punish, but also He is forgiving and merciful.

(Surah 6: 165)

Muslims believe that human beings were given the role of *khalifah* or guardian/steward to look after the earth and treat it with respect.

This responsibility is a binding duty on the whole community of Muslims (*ummah*). Muslims come from many countries and speak a wide range of languages, but they were all created by Allah and are expected to follow the *Shariah* (the Islamic law based on the Qur'an and Sunnah).

Muslims are expected to actively keep the delicate natural balance of the environment – the key to survival. This is considered such an important role that on the Day of Judgement, all Muslims will be called into account for how they have looked after Allah's creation.

Creation in Hinduism

Hindus believe that Creation is *anadi* (that which has no beginning) and that it is eternal. The concern with the cosmic forces is described in the second book of the Upanishads. Here there are references to how balance is maintained through vast and continuous sacrifice. The five elements – ether, air, water, earth, and fire – are all engaged in continual sacrifice. The world of plants sacrifices itself to animals, animals to one another and to humans, and so on. So it is human's self-sacrifice which sustains their children. In this way there is a never-ending destruction and renewal of all life and matter. A verse in the Rig Veda describes the sacrifice of Purusha, the Cosmic Man, likening the elements of the sacrifice to the seasons:

When God prepared the sacrifice with Purusha as their offering,
Its oils was spring, the holy gift was autumn,
Summer was the wood.
They balmed as victim on the grass,
Purusha,
Born in earliest time ...

It is believed that this is just one of the many universes which have been created.

At the end of the last age there was a great deluge which destroyed the universe. Brahma, the creator, prayed to Brahman to create a new universe. It is believed that when Brahma sleeps, then nothing exists. When he awakes then the world takes shape.

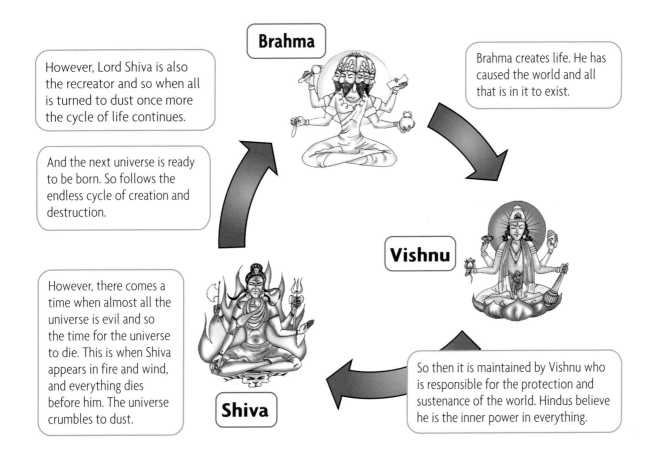

Brahma

However, Lord Shiva is also the recreator and so when all is turned to dust once more the cycle of life continues.

And the next universe is ready to be born. So follows the endless cycle of creation and destruction.

Brahma creates life. He has caused the world and all that is in it to exist.

Vishnu

However, there comes a time when almost all the universe is evil and so the time for the universe to die. This is when Shiva appears in fire and wind, and everything dies before him. The universe crumbles to dust.

Shiva

So then it is maintained by Vishnu who is responsible for the protection and sustenance of the world. Hindus believe he is the inner power in everything.

The Big Bang Theory

Many people feel that this theory is a little more acceptable than creation to scientific thinking.

This theory, as its name suggests, states that everything began with a big bang. The dense matter that made up the universe began to expand about 15,000 million years ago, bursting out with great force and speed. Since then, the expansion has continued, with a gradual cooling down of the earth and other planets.

The knowledge we have of the universe seems to confirm this theory, as the stars in the universe are all burning masses, just like our sun. They also have planets grouped around them in galaxies, all moving apart and cooling down.

Whether this expanding continues for ever, or eventually begins contracting again until there is another big bang is uncertain, and people have differing views about it.

> St Thomas Aquinas believed:
>
> ' Everything that happens has a cause. If we follow each cause back we come to a First Cause that started everything off. That First Cause is God. '

> Professor J. Wickramasinghe stated:
>
> ' The idea that life was put together by random shuffling is as ridiculous and improbable as the idea that a tornado blowing through a junk yard may assemble a Boeing 747. The aircraft had a creator and so has life. '

Two important things to note about the Big Bang idea:

- It is only a theory, and some scientists do not accept some of the evidence and question its accuracy

- There are some unanswerable questions about the theory, such as 'what caused the bang?' and 'where did the matter come from in the first place?'

Many Christians are happy to accept the principle of the Big Bang, and understand God as the cause of the Bang.

Some think it unnecessary to ask who caused it, but we should just acknowledge that it happened, and that the principle of cause and effect we now recognise in the world has come about through the processes following the explosion.

Only one of these moths is likely to survive in this environment.

> Did God really create humans? Or did he just begin the process?

> Are humans really unique? Or are they just evolved apes, and therefore just like any other animal?

The Theory of Evolution

Another scientific theory that raises questions about belief in creation is Darwin's theory of the origins of life – or evolution. During the 19th century, when investigating the distribution of animals in the islands of the Southern Hemisphere, Charles Darwin noticed how animals had adapted to changes in their environment. He was able to show clearly that changes in the physical make up of animals resulted from a process of natural selection. This was where the best and fittest survived and passed on their characteristics to a new generation.

It was this principle Darwin suggested in his book *The Origin of the Species*, that over millions of years changes have been occuring, and the complex forms of life existing today are likely to have evolved from simpler and earlier forms of life.

To many, this raises doubts about God's role in creation, as it seems that species evolved from one thing to another over time in a process that happened through natural selection rather than divine intervention. The idea also suggests that human beings, rather than being created in God's image, had evolved from apes, and were merely a more complex and rational version.

On the other hand, many religious believers see no real conflict at all, as they either believe God established the process of natural selection as the means for life to evolve, or that evolution is a process that God is involved in from time to time so as to bring about a significant change or development.

It is important to note the following points about the theory of evolution:

- It is a theory, and has not been proved absolutely

- It describes a process of development and adaptation within species – the question is still not completely clear about transformation from one species to another

- It does not explain the origins of the first life forms

- It does not explain the order in the universe, or the reason for 'natural laws' that exist within the universe.

Science and Religion

All these issues raise questions about the relationship between science and religion.

Are they complementary?

Science and religion do not go against each other; they answer different questions, and together give us a bigger picture.

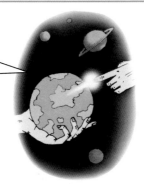

Can a scientist be a Christian? Can a Christian accept scientific reasoning?

Do they conflict?

6 Science without religion is lame; religion without science is blind. 9

(Albert Einstein)

6 I have faith in the Mathematics I teach, even though it is all based on unprovable axioms. I have a far more important faith ... in the living God ... (the reality of God's existence is a 'self-evident truth') 9

Anne Sweeney, Lecturer in Mathematics

6 Science and religion seek to answer different questions. Science asks how things happen, religion asks why. Genesis is not there to give us strict, technical answers about how the universe began. It gives us the big answer that things exist because of God's will. One can perfectly well believe in the Big Bang but believe it as the will of God the creator. 9

(John Polkinghorne, Professor of Mathematical Physics, University of Cambridge)

John Polkinghorne

Really, science and religion are **both** asking questions about the world and life; they are however asking different kinds of questions.

Simply put, science asks **how** questions:

Why?

- How did this begin?
- How can we explain this?
- How did this actually happen?

Religion asks **why** questions:
- Why did this begin?
- Why are we here?
- Why did this happen?

How?

So we can say that religious and scientific views on creation or the beginnings of life differ as follows:

Religious views:	Scientific views:
● Try to explain the purpose in things that happen;	● Try to explain how and when things happen;
● Explain the value or significance;	● Explain the mechanisms and processes;
● Start from general beliefs and work to the particular;	● Start from the particular and work to the general principles they suggest;
● Are statements of belief based on sacred writings, religious experience and/or tradition;	● Are hypotheses based on evidence collected and the extant knowledge available;
● Are not open to categorical or empirical proof or disproof;	● Are open to review or rejection as new or wider information becomes available;
● Are sometimes taken to be 'literal' truths; though many understand them as parables, allegories or myths of explanation.	● Are explanations of how things are seen and believed to be, and are not considered to be religious, philosophical or metaphysical in nature.

 **Exam Tip**

How to do Evaluative Questions

Try to follow the simple guide opposite, and so make sure that you deal with all aspects of this type of question; you will then find you meet the criteria of the Levels of Response Grid for AO 3 questions, as shown on page 117.

What?	Ask yourself, 'What is the statement saying?'	*Read it carefully.*
Agree?	Say what you think for yourself. You can say, 'Yes, I agree' or 'No, I do not agree' or 'I partly agree and partly disagree'.	*Be clear and precise in what you say.*
Why?	Give reasons and/or evidence to support your view. Try and include religious arguments or issues here if you can.	*Say why you have the view you have stated.*
On the other hand?	Think about other views – not necessarily just the opposite view! Comment on them sensitively, and try to include religious ideas here if you haven't already done so.	*Make sure you consider other views or ideas.*
So?	Round off your answer by coming to a conclusion, referring back to the statement in the question.	*End off with a clear conclusion to your answer.*

Q *'Believing that the world was created is not in line with modern knowledge.' Do you agree? Give reasons or evidence for your answer, showing that you have thought about more than one point of view.* [6]

Look at this example. The candidate has clearly read the question carefully, asking what is it about.

AGREE?
A clear statement of view is given.

WHY?
Reasons for the view taken are clearly given, including some religious ideas/issues, and also consideration of other views.

ON THE OTHER HAND?
An alternative view is considered with sensitivity and a showing that such a view also has reasons behind it.

SO?
A conclusion is made, with a clear reference back to the statement in the question.

I do not agree with the statement, although I do understand why some people may make such statements.

The reason I disagree is that religious views about the beginning of the universe do not necessarily try to explain the practical details, but more the purpose and reason. So, Christians who believe that God created the world are actually underlining four key things: 1 that everything was created for a purpose; 2 that life's beginnings were not accidental; 3 that humans are different from animals; and 4 the world was basically good.

Likewise, scientific views try to explain the mechanisms and processes, but are only hypotheses based on current evidence and knowledge, and are open to being re-written later on when more or new knowledge becomes available. As such, they are not as certain or authoritative as some would believe.

Of course, there are those who believe that scientific knowledge and understanding of the world has displaced most of traditional religious views on creation. They are convinced that studies and research give sufficient evidence to reject religious views. So the ability to study things in microscopic detail, and to collate all the information gathered using modern technology, raises serious questions for them about religious creation stories and beliefs.

However, I feel that religion and science need not be seen to be in conflict. Once a person realises that they are answering different kinds of questions, we can find they both have something to offer to our wider understanding of our universe. I do not, though, accept that belief in creation is either out of step with modern knowledge or an indication that a believer is not willing to take account of modern scientific research and investigation.

Now do your own evaluation question using the **WAWOS** framework.

How should we care for the world?

Who Made a Mess?

Who made a mess of the planet
And what's that bad smell in the breeze?
Who punched a hole in the ozone
And who took an axe to my trees?

Who sprayed the garden with poison
While trying to scare off a fly?
Who streaked the water with oil slicks
And who let my fish choke and die?

Who tossed that junk in the river
And who stained the fresh air with fumes?
Who tore the fields with a digger
And who blocked my favourite views?

Who's going to tidy up later
And who's going to find what you've lost?
Who's going to say that they're sorry
And who's going to carry the cost?

(Steve Turner)

Handle with care

❝ We are facing an environmental crisis. The planet is more threatened by the danger to its life systems than it has ever been through war. ❞

Maurice Strong
Secretary General, United Nations Committee
on Environment and Development

Some people in the past have felt that our '**dominion**' over the world and other animals gave them the right to exploit the world and all in it for their own personal advantage.

For many years, humans have plundered the world and the environment, and are now beginning to recognise the importance of responsible management of the earth's resources and its environment.

> **DOMINION** – a word meaning 'kingship', or 'being the boss over something'. The Bible story of creation says humans were given 'dominion' over the world and its creatures, and for most of them it means 'being in charge of the world for God'.

Christianity ✚

Christians would say that if humans learn to live sensibly and in true partnership with God and his creation, then they find nature itself responds and people come closer to God as they praise him for all he has provided.

Christians try to remind themselves that God did not only create the world in the beginning, but that his hand is still at work in the natural cycle of the world and its seasons.

So they remind themselves regularly, in worship and celebrations, of God's provision and their own responsibility too. (E.g. harvest thanksgiving; grace before meals.)

There are many organisations and individuals who work to protect the earth. Many humans, because of religious or moral teachings, feel they have a **RESPONSIBILITY** to care for the earth and the environment. Many people feel they are partners with God in looking after the world.

Christians use the term **STEWARDSHIP** to explain this responsibility.

Check it out

What is stewardship?

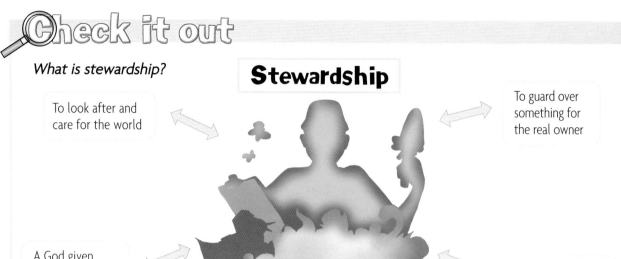

Stewardship

To look after and care for the world

To guard over something for the real owner

A God given responsibility to manage or control the earth

Carefully looking after something that is not your own

An example of a Christian steward:

CHICO MENDES

Situation: In Brazil there had been environmental problems. Huge hardwood trees were being chopped down to make furniture and buildings. Mercury was being used to help separate the gold from the land. This had another effect of polluting the water, and so killing the fish and anyone drinking the water. Rain forests were being burnt down to make space for crops and livestock. After three years the land had become exhausted, barren, and then become abandoned. Many people living there just wanted the area to be left alone.

Who was Chico Mendes?

Chico was a leader of the rubber tappers. He had been a rubber tapper since the age of nine years. As a rubber tapper he had not been able to go to school. Later in his life he organised the rubber tappers to defend their homes from cattle ranchers. From the 1970s he organised non-violent resistance to the exploitation of the forests. He found ways to use Amazonian resources to support the

economic benefit for the local people and to protect the rainforest from logging and cattle ranching.

In 1988 he led a winning effort to stop cattle ranchers from deforesting an area the rubber tappers wanted to make into a reserve.

CHICO MENDES THREATENED THE **SUCCESS** OF BIG LANDOWNERS AND BUSINESS INTERESTS WHO STAND TO MAKE **ENORMOUS** PROFITS FROM THE **WHOLESALE** DESTRUCTION OF THE FOREST.

He was killed outside his house later that year by the son of a cattle rancher.

In his memory, the land he lived and died for – the 970,570,000 hectares – was named the Chico Mendes Extractive Reserve.

CHICO WAS **SHOT DEAD** ON THE BACK DOORSTEP OF HIS HOUSE, IN FRONT OF HIS WIFE AND YOUNG FAMILY.

 Look it up http://www.chicomendes.com
http://www.edj.org/programs/International/Chico

 Exam Tip

In some questions – especially about the environment – it may be possible to answer almost entirely by stating general ideas, rather than religious beliefs or teachings. It is perfectly acceptable to include general ideas, but if the questions asks for the beliefs or teachings of a religion, be sure to include them in your answer.

 Q *Describe the teaching of **one** religious tradition about caring for the world and the environment.* [6]

Look at the two answers below. One has been given a Level 1 and 2 marks; the other a Level 4 and 5 marks. Can you work out which, and why?

Answer A	Answer B
Name of religious tradition: Christianity	Name of religious tradition: Islam
Teaching on caring for the world and its environment: Humans are responsible for caring for the world as it is them who pollute the environment. So they should clean it up, or they won't have a world to live in anyway. They have the power and the means to look after it, so they should.	Teaching on caring for the world and its environment: Muslims believe that Allah made the world and all that is in it. Humans are the most important, and are believed to be khalifahs. As such they should use their talents and intelligence to look after the world and care for the environment. Muslims believe that people will be asked questions on judgement day about how much they have done for the world.

Islam ☪

Muslims believe that Allah created, owns and sustains the world and all its creatures. The creation is considered as a whole, of which plants, animals and humans are a part. This is just like the *ummah* where all Muslim believers, irrespective of race, age or background, are seen as part of a whole. Every human is believed to have a special role as a *khalifah* to protect the environment.

> He has made
> you His ruling agents
> in the earth
>
> (Surah 6: 165)

> **UMMAH** — the community of Muslim believers

> **KHALIFAH** — agent or steward working for Allah

> **FITRAH** — balance in the natural world

Adam's children are the limbs of
    one another
For in creation, they are from one
    substance
When time causes pain to one limb
The other limbs cannot rest
If you do not care for the afflictions
    of others
You do not deserve to be called a
    human being

(Verse from a poem by the Sufi poet, Sadi)

The survival of the planet depends upon maintaining the natural *fitrah* and realising the interdependency on each other. There are many examples of where the earth has been damaged by deforestation and the extinction of species of animals. Muslims consider it a duty to use their skills to help keep the balance which Allah created.

In Islam, the more that one possesses, the more one should ensure its ethical use. This responsibility is so serious that on the Day of Judgement Muslims believe they will need to answer to Allah how they have treated the earth and all living creatures. The Prophet Muhammad set an example of the care that should be given to the natural world, showing kindness to animals is considered an important act. All animals and insects are part of Allah's creation – no matter how big or small! He often spoke of the importance of planting trees and gardens from which birds, animals and humans could benefit. There are many examples in the Hadith (Sayings of Muhammad) of how the Prophet avoided waste, was kind to animals, and respected the earth.

How the Prophet Muhammad showed the importance of all creation:	
In his sayings:	*In his actions:*
❛The whole earth has been created a place of worship, pure and clean❜ (respect the earth)	On a long journey, Muhammad and some travelling companions lit a fire to keep themselves warm. The Prophet then realised that nearby was an anthill, and the ants were running in the direction of the fire. Muhammad had the fire immediately extinguished.
❛Live in this world as if you were going to live forever❜ (don't waste resources)	One day the Prophet passed by a camel that had been mistreated. He taught the listening people, *'Fear Allah in these beasts – ride them in good health and free them from work while they are still in good health.'*

Interview with Safia, a Muslim

Safia is a 16-year-old Muslim girl living in Cardiff. She was born in England and is studying at school for her GCSEs. Safia is trying to convince her friend Helen to be more environmentally friendly.

Safia: Helen, you've left the taps on again! Have you any idea how much water you are wasting? Water is precious you know.

Helen: That's fine, coming from you. Have you ever thought how much water you waste getting washed before prayers?

Safia: It's called wudu, and we always make sure we only use the minimum. In fact, at the mosque, all the taps are controlled so that they only let a little water out. Prophet Muhammad said we must not waste water, even if we lived near a river. The teachers in the *madrassah* [mosque school] are always concerned about how we look after the environment. Last year, the Mosque won a 'Cardiff in Bloom' competition for the care we took with our garden.

Helen: Why do you have a garden? At our church we have a graveyard. Does that count?

Safia: The Prophet Muhammad often spoke about the beauties of a garden. After a hard day at school, I like to go to the garden because it helps me remember that Allah is the creator, and that I have been given the responsibility to act as a *khalifah*, or guardian.

Helen: What do you mean 'guardian'? You're only sixteen! What can you do to help the world?

Safia: A lot! As a Muslim I have a commitment to the whole Muslim community – the *ummah*. It is a duty for me to make sure that I respect the environment and make sure I treat animals as a part of Allah's creation.

Helen: But how can you say that when you eat meat? If you cared for animals you would be a vegetarian.

Safia: Well, there are certain meats, such as pork, that I am not allowed to eat, but all the animals must be killed in the quickest and kindest way possible. We never take food for granted. When we fast during the month of Ramadan, it reminds us of how precious food is. After the fast we are always grateful for the food we believe Allah has provided.

 **Look it up** http://www.ifees.org

21

Judaism

The Earth is the Lord's and the fullness thereof

(Psalm 24: 1)

Jews believe they have a duty to look after the world which God has created, and which is only loaned to humans.

There are many ways Jews will carry out their responsibilities, but they can be summed up as:

- **T**hanksgiving
- **L**itter-free
- **C**oncern.

Thanksgiving

There are many festivals in the Jewish calendar, and many of the celebrations concern thanking God for the environment.

Sukkot – This festival comes in the autumn months and many Jews build a *sukkah* in their garden or at their synagogue. This is a building like a booth in which, during the festival, some families will eat their meals or even sleep. The walls are made of canvas or thin board, and the roof will be made from leafy branches through which it will be possible to see the sky. Staying in the sukkah reminds people how they are dependent on God and his creation.

Tu B'Shevat – At this festival it is remembered how important trees are for all human existence. As part of the celebration young trees are often planted.

Litter-free

Jews believe it is important that there is no waste, and try to ensure that in their own lifestyle.

Concern

It is expected that animals will be treated with concern and compassion, as they too are part of God's creation. Most Jews do not agree with hunting, and care should be taken that when an animal is slaughtered it should be done as painlessly as possible.

Joy Fifer

A 60 year-old member of the Birmingham Progressive Synagogue is fighting not only for her own life, but for the lives of animals as well.

Joy Fifer, who has been waiting for a lung transplant for two years, is spearheading a campaign through the national Jewish environmental group Noah, to ban fox-hunting.

Mrs Fifer explained: 'The Jewish position is quite clear. The principle of *tsa'ar ba'alei chayim* – the prevention of animals' suffering – and *ba'al tashlich* – you shall not destroy – clearly would apply to the so-called sport of fox-hunting.'

The Jewish National Fund

Many Jewish homes and shops will show their support of the environment by putting charity money in their blue Jewish National Fund collecting box. The first blue collecting boxes were used in 1904, and since then money raised in them has bought 12.5% of all land in Israel.

Blue Box

Originally a large part of the funds was used to develop the land by planting trees. In recent years more attention is being given to the importance of providing water.

Look it up
http://www.jnf.co.uk/

THE JNF UNVEILS PLANS FOR A £4 MILLION WATER PROJECT IN ISRAEL

The project comes three months after the JNF completed its five-year Besor reservoir project in the Negev. With a capacity of 4 million cubic metres of water, it is the largest in the Middle East.

'Water is Israel's most vital resource, and the key to evenly distributing Israel's ever-growing population is to ensure there is a ready supply of it – for drinking and agriculture,' said JNF chief executive, Simon Winters.

Hinduism ॐ

As Hindus believe that all living beings have *atman*, so they consider all life to be precious and sacred, and should not be harmed.

All animals are to be respected but special honour is given to the cow, who provides milk and butter, and works in the fields. The respect they give to the cow reflects their thankfulness to the earth.

This belief in non-violence is called **AHIMSA**, and means 'to have reverence for all life'. Many Hindus show *ahimsa* by being vegetarians, and refusing to eat any part of an animal that has been slaughtered.

Some Hindus also refuse to eat eggs, as they could become living beings.

ATMAN – Self; usually refers to the real self, the soul

Vrindavan

Vrindavan lies eighty miles south of Delhi and is particularly important to many Hindus as it was here that Krishna was born and lived. By the 1980s most of the trees had been cut down, having an effect on the environment and animals.

For every hair on the body of a beast, the person who kills it without reason will be slaughtered in successive births.

(Manu 5, 38)

With support from the World Wildlife Fund, the Vrindavan Forest Revival Project organised a major tree-planting programme, as well as educational projects. Recent developments have included the cleaning of the Yamuna River.

THE VRINDAVAN DECLARATION

Nature enjoys being enjoyed, but reacts furiously to exploitation. Today's situation is caused by our separation from Krishna and his message of commitment. Let us act on his message to play, not to exploit

Look it up

www.mathura-vrindavan.com/
www.vrindavan.com/vrnda01.html

Exam Tip

Within many units you will be expected to know about the impact of the work of one individual or agency. In this unit you will be expected to have a knowledge and understanding of one agency or individual that has used their particular talents to help care for the environment. There are a number of questions you should ask yourself – these are shown below.

Who Should I Choose?

The person or agency you refer to may be local, national or international. It may be someone you have studied as a class or that you have a particular interest in.

Remember the Specification requires your study to be from particular faith beliefs. **You must make sure the person/agency you have chosen is from one of the religions you are studying.**

What Do I Need To Know?

You will be expected to show in your answer what the person or agency:

1 **does** to care for the earth;
2 **why** they have this concern, and
3 **what** their religious inspirations are.

You do not need to know a list of dates or family details. **Your answers should show that you have an understanding of the IMPACT of their work.**

Where Will I Get My Information From?

You may take your particular study as a class lesson or be expected to conduct your own research. The amount of detail you need to know depends upon whether you are using the information to answer an exam question or part of a piece of coursework. Whichever, you should refer to **as wide a range as possible**.

Web sites – many agencies and individuals have informative websites. You will find some useful examples in the 'Look It Up' boxes in this book.

Newspapers – you may find relevant information in daily newspapers. Many religions have their own newspapers or magazines, such as: *Catholic Herald*, *Jewish Chronicle*, *Q News*.

Publicity materials – often an agency will produce videos or booklets describing the work they do and any current events.

Interviews – if a local person or agency is your focus, then you may be able to conduct your own interview.

Range of books – do not rely on just one book, use a number of them to get a wider picture.

Task

- Select one person or agency who has used their talents to care for the environment. Then fill in the following framework. **Remember to be precise.** The whole answer should illustrate the **IMPACT** of their work.

Identify the correct name of the person or agency.

Mention the religious tradition to which they belong.

Précis the context in which the person or agency is working.

Acknowledge some of the main aspects of their work.

Consider how their work demonstrates the teachings of the religion to which they belong.

Tell of specific examples of the long and short term projects.

TEST IT OUT

Here is a typical set of examination questions for this unit.
Write out answers to them, trying to take account of the Exam Tips
and information you have been given.

(a) In addition to 'having dominion … over all the earth' (Genesis 1: 26), what do Christians believe are the other main purposes of humans being on the earth? [4]

(b) What is 'stewardship'? [2]

(c) What are the differences between a religious view of creation (or the beginning of the universe) and scientific views? You may answer from any religious tradition. [6]

(d) Describe the teaching of **one** religious tradition about the human 'soul' or 'spirit'. [4]

(e) State **two** ways in which human beings have spoiled the world. [2]

(f) 'Humans aren't very intelligent because they are destroying their own world.' Do you agree? Give reasons and evidence for your answer, showing that you have thought about more than one point of view. [6]

2 Relationships

What commitments and responsibilities do we have?

We have many different types of relationships with other people:

my grandparents

my parents

my brother/sister

my neighbours

my uncles/aunts

my boy/girl friend

my nieces/nephews

my work mates

my cousins

my school friends

my teachers

my faith community/friends/members

The relationships are all different, and we respond differently to each of the people.

- What do you think your **responsibilities** are to:
  a) your parents?
  b) your relatives?
  c) your friends?
  d) your neighbours?

- Choose two or three of the above, and write down what kind of **commitments** you make to those people.

Check it out

Responsibility

Duties you should carry out

Liabilities

Your obligations

What you are expected to take care of

Something you do out of a sense of duty, or because you are expected to do it.

Check it out

Commitment

Dedication towards something or someone

Being devoted towards someone or something

Making AND keeping a promise

Keeping an obligation

Something you choose to do, or be, for a person

Something you want to do, or be, perhaps because of something else you have already chosen for yourself

 Exam Tip

When giving an answer that requires a definition, be precise in what you say. Many candidates do not gain full marks because they repeat words or phrases within their answer, or because they do not cover the essential points of a definition.

 Q *Explain the meaning of 'commitment' when used about a relationship.* [2]

Look at the two answers below and you will see a full answer and a part answer.

Answer A	Answer B
Devotion	Being completely devoted to another person, because you want to, and perhaps because you love that person or are married to them.

Most people develop special relationships with particular individuals.

Friends – these may be people of either sex with whom we have a lot in common, and we like to spend time with them.

Boyfriend/Girlfriend – this is a particular person for whom we develop a very close friendship.

Some people would describe their feelings with the word 'love'.

What is 'love'?

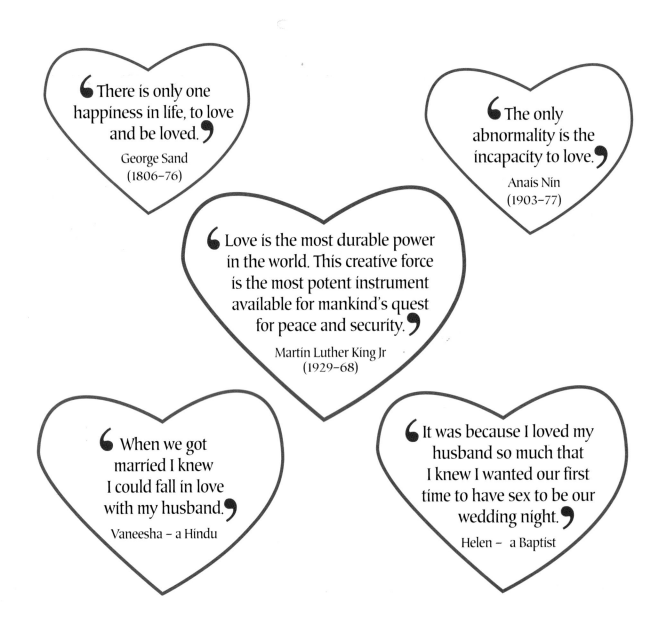

' There is only one happiness in life, to love and be loved. '
George Sand
(1806–76)

' The only abnormality is the incapacity to love. '
Anaïs Nin
(1903–77)

' Love is the most durable power in the world. This creative force is the most potent instrument available for mankind's quest for peace and security. '
Martin Luther King Jr
(1929–68)

' When we got married I knew I could fall in love with my husband. '
Vaneesha – a Hindu

' It was because I loved my husband so much that I knew I wanted our first time to have sex to be our wedding night. '
Helen – a Baptist

Most religions have teachings about marriage and sex before marriage. Believers from each tradition will refer to these teachings when making their decisions about personal relationships.

Christianity	Hinduism	Islam	Judaism
• begins the special relationship between two people. • the couple will usually be in love when they marry, but expect to develop that love. • marriage consists of one man to one woman at any one time. • considered a sacrament – a relationship in which God himself is involved. • sex should generally take place within marriage. • sex is a gift from God, and is holy and sacred; it is special and should be reserved between just two people at any one time/period in one's life. • casual sex or promiscuity is seen as devaluing both people and sex, and therefore unacceptable. • bringing-up of children is an important part of marriage.	• within the system of *varnashramadharma* the students must exercise chastity until the end of their studies. • marriage consists of one man to one woman. • begins the relationship between two extended families not just the individuals. • considered a sacrament – *samskara.* • begins the householder stage, and a new set of duties. • usually love is expected to grow and develop. • sex should only happen within marriage. • *kama* (sensual pleasure) is one of the four Hindu aims of life. • bringing-up of children is an important part of marriage.	• begins the relationship between two extended families not just the individuals. • marriage is a social contract which has Allah's sanction. • it is not a sacrament but a legal binding contract between man and woman. • sex should only happen within marriage. • couples are expected to meet each other's needs. • sex is considered an act of worship. • bringing up of children is an important part of marriage. • polygamy (marriage of a man to more than one wife) is allowed in exceptional circumstances, and when the law of the land allows.	• begins the contract between two people with God's blessing. • the couple will usually be in love when they marry, but expect that love to develop. • marriage consists of one man to one woman at any one time. • just like Adam and Eve, the couple should be a support for each other. • sex is expected only to take place within marriage. • sex is seen as one of the three stages of marriage – betrothal/ contract/ consummation. • bringing up of children is an important part of marriage.

Some people choose a **celibate** lifestyle. Sometimes this choice has been made to allow people to dedicate their lives to serving God. Those taking Holy Orders in the Roman Catholic Church are expected to remain celibate.

CELIBATE – deciding never to have a sexual relationship

Exam Tip

Many things seem the same. Check out similarities and differences between the two religious traditions you are studying. Remember to be specific in your answers – do not use a 'cover-all' type of answer.

Q *Describe why people marry in **two** religious traditions.* [4]

- Correct this answer:

> In my two religions, the couples get married because they love each other. They often want to have children. And live happily ever after.

Religious traditions believe making sex something special within only a marriage relationship is not a negative thing, but is actually very positive:

Celebrates the **JOY** of sex	It is a celebration of the joy of sex as a mutual partnership – a complete giving of oneself totally and personally to another.
Highlights the **RESPONSIBILITY**	It is a highlighting of responsibility towards another person – a thinking about them and their needs, not just a satisfying of one's own needs.
States the place of **COMMITMENT**	It is a stating of the importance of commitment in their relationship – a willingness to spend the rest of one's life with someone you love.
Adds a **SPIRITUAL DIMENSION**	It is an enhancing of the relationship by including a religious and spiritual dimension – an understanding that the sexual relationship is not just physical uniting, but a spiritual and religious experience too.
Strengthens the legal side or **CONTRACT**	It strengthens the relationship as it becomes part of a legal and social joining of two lives – and ensures that both partners have clear rights should things go wrong.

ONE THING SHE WILL NOT DO

Britney Spears is one of many people who has declared she will remain chaste until she is married. The True Love Waits International movement involves hundreds of thousands of young people pledging themselves to be chaste until marriage.

 **Look it up** www.truelovewaits.com/index.htm

In the same way, sex outside of marriage is not acceptable to most Christians. Having kept themselves for each other before marriage, and given themselves unreservedly to each other, there should be no desire or willingness to look for sexual relationships or experiences outside of the marriage. This is known as **fidelity**. This means that Christians have clear guidelines about adultery, or having a sexual relationship with someone other than one's marriage partner.

> **FIDELITY** – fidelity is a keeping of oneself sexually loyal to one's partner, just as chastity was a keeping of oneself as a virgin until marriage.

Christian teaching about adultery:

- marriage is sexually exclusive – sex should not be shared with anyone else (the special relationship [or 'one-ness'] is destroyed)

- is forbidden in the 10 commandments and teaching of Jesus

- is harmful to the special relationship of marriage

- is not a secure basis for any children born as a result

- could result in a partner feeling cheated, betrayed, or rejected

- is wrong because God himself is involved in the marriage (sacrament).

Against The 10 Commandments
Damages lives
Undermines marriage
Lets others down
Trust is broken
Ends family security
Relationships harmed
You'd best avoid it!

Hindu teaching about adultery:

- Marriage is a religious duty – a *samskara* – so the ideals of it are too, and will produce good *karma*.

- Hindu scriptures and society approve only of sex within marriage, and so chastity is encouraged prior to marriage, and fidelity within marriage.

- A vow or promise of faithfulness is made in the 7th step of the ceremony, and is seen as a lifelong commitment.

- Faithfulness to one's partner in marriage is depicted by Sita in the Ramayana.

- The *yamas* (5 abstentions) and *Niyamas* (5 observances) preclude adultery: *Yama* – lying, lust, greed; *Niyama* – purity, patience, contentment.

Islamic teaching about adultery:

- Sex outside of marriage is generally strongly disapproved of.

- Sexual desires are to be satisfied, but only in the context of marriage.

- The ideal is a lifelong union based on trust, morality and devotion.

- Vows promising to be faithful are exchanged in the marriage ceremony.

- Adultery is seen as harmful socially, so against the unity and peace of the *Ummah*.

- Adultery is seen as a form of theft of the worst possible sort: *'Have nothing to do with adultery, for it is a shameful thing and an evil opening the way to other evils'* (Surah 17: 32)

Jewish teaching about adultery:

- The 10 Commandments specifically forbid adultery *'You shall not commit adultery'* (Exodus 20:13).

- Sex is only acceptable within marriage – a stable relationship between one man and one woman.

- *Halakhah* (code of conduct) emphasises that a husband should be sexually considerate towards his wife; and this precludes disloyalty sexually.

- Men and women are most fulfilled through marriage, which is referred to as '*kiddushim*' (sanctified)

Task

- Answer this question.

Q *People who marry as virgins will have a stronger bond of trust and commitment.' Do you agree? Give reasons or evidence for your answer, showing that you have thought about more than one point of view.* [6]

Remember to use the WAWOS formula *[What? Agree? Why? On the other hand? So?] (page 14).*

So what happens?

If sex is to be kept until marriage, then marriage is being seen as a special event, and most religions have views about and ceremonies for marriage.

But marriage is by no means the only possibility:

Religious Marriage Ceremonies

Remember, within all religious traditions, couples with their families will choose the actual content of their marriage ceremony.

Christian Marriage Ceremony

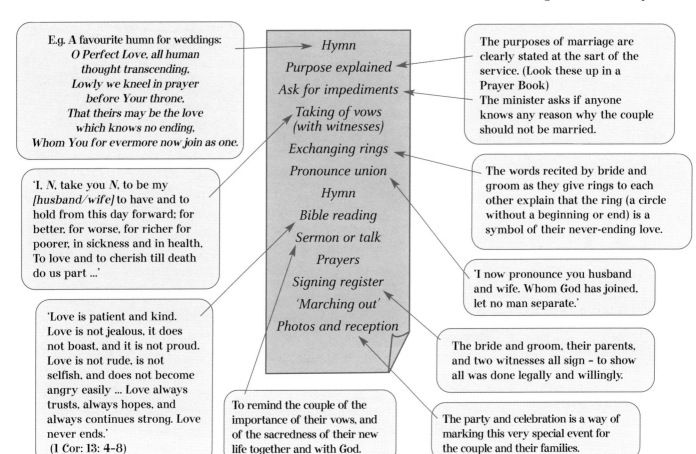

E.g. A favourite humn for weddings:
O Perfect Love, all human
thought transcending,
Lowly we kneel in prayer
before Your throne,
That theirs may be the love
which knows no ending,
Whom You for evermore now join as one.

'I, *N*, take you *N*, to be my *[husband/wife]* to have and to hold from this day forward; for better, for worse, for richer for poorer, in sickness and in health, To love and to cherish till death do us part ...'

'Love is patient and kind. Love is not jealous, it does not boast, and it is not proud. Love is not rude, is not selfish, and does not become angry easily ... Love always trusts, always hopes, and always continues strong. Love never ends.'
(1 Cor: 13: 4–8)

Hymn
Purpose explained
Ask for impediments
Taking of vows (with witnesses)
Exchanging rings
Pronounce union
Hymn
Bible reading
Sermon or talk
Prayers
Signing register
'Marching out'
Photos and reception

The purposes of marriage are clearly stated at the sart of the service. (Look these up in a Prayer Book)
The minister asks if anyone knows any reason why the couple should not be married.

The words recited by bride and groom as they give rings to each other explain that the ring (a circle without a beginning or end) is a symbol of their never-ending love.

'I now pronounce you husband and wife. Whom God has joined, let no man separate.'

The bride and groom, their parents, and two witnesses all sign – to show all was done legally and willingly.

To remind the couple of the importance of their vows, and of the sacredness of their new life together and with God.

The party and celebration is a way of marking this very special event for the couple and their families.

Christianity

Before a marriage takes place there is likely to be a lot of preparation for the big day: arrangements for the service, the bride's and brides-maids' dresses, the flowers, and of course the reception afterwards. The ceremony itself will usually take place in a church or chapel, because for believing Christians, marriage is a sacrament, and there are religious elements that they would want in their special day. For others, marriage in a church is mainly for the setting, and sometimes marriages are arranged in a registry office, or a hotel, or some other place.

Hinduism ॐ

Before a Hindu wedding takes place there will have been much preparation. Parents and the extended family will have assisted by searching for suitable partners. The families will then have arranged for the couple to have supervised meetings after which they will decide whether to continue the relationship or not. If the couple feel the relationship is promising then they will consult a priest who will look at their horoscopes to see if they are compatible.

The process is often called an '**arranged marriage**' but most Hindus would prefer to call

it an '***assisted marriage***'. Within the majority of families today, the couple themselves take a lead role in the arrangements with the family assisting or supporting the proceedings.

The wedding ceremony itself is considered by many Hindus to be one of the **samskaras** or rites of passage which begins a new stage of life. The ceremony itself can take place in a hall or *mandir*. Often a decorated *mandip* or canopy is erected under which the ceremony will take place. There are many important and symbolic aspects of the ceremony. Offerings to Ganesha – who it's believed can remove obstacles that can be put in the way of a marriage. A havan (fire) is lit and offerings of incense sprinkled into the flames. Agreement of the couple is asked for. The bride's scarf is tied to the groom's and they circle the fire. The bride places her toe on a stone to show her obedience and loyalty to her husband. Seven steps are taken around the fire for food, strength, wealth, happiness, children, long wedded life, and unity. During the ceremony, commitments to *dharma* (religious duty), *artha* (economic development) and *kama* (sense of enjoyment) will be made.

Islam

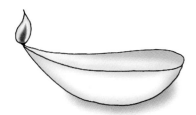

Before a Muslim marriage takes place there will have been much preparation. Within Islam it is believed important to allow the whole family to assist with the finding of the right partner. This is a practice which is often referred to as **arranged** or assisted marriages. This will include parents searching for a suitable partner which may then lead to the prospective couple meeting. From the meeting the couple will consider whether to continue with the relationship or to decide they are not compatible.

If they decide to continue, the *mahr* or dowry is arranged. This is the payment of an agreed sum of money to the wife. The money belongs to the wife, and is hers to keep should they later decide to divorce.

The ceremony which means the couple are married under Islamic law is called the *Nikah*, and may take place at home, in the mosque or anywhere else where the witnesses (often including an *imam* or leader) are present. The bride does not have to be present, but must send witnesses. Usually the ceremony will include:

● Recitation of *ayahs* (units of surahs from the Qur'an)
● Agreement to the *mahr* in front of witnesses
● Exchange of vows
● Signing the contract.

Judaism

The marriage ceremony will usually be held in a synagogue, but can also be held in the open air. The format will differ depending upon whether the bride and groom are Liberal, Reform, or Orthodox Jews. The ceremony can take place on any day except *Shabbat* and festivals. Often there will have been a lot of preparation before:

● Lessons with the rabbi, to help the couple understand the importance of marriage

● Fasting before the ceremony to help prepare the couple for a solemn time.

The ceremony is held under a **chuppah** (canopy) – which is often decorated with flowers – and supported by four poles. The groom and the bride stand under the chuppah with other close relatives joining them during the service.

There are many important aspects of the ceremony which normally include the following:

● Blessings of wine and marriage
● Exchange of rings
● Music from the choir
● Sermon from the rabbi
● Signing the *ketubah* or marriage document
● Final seven blessings
● Breaking of the wine glass, to symbolise the fragility of marriage and the destruction of the Temple.

 Exam Tip

You must try to remember to include specific religious content in your answers to questions about the teaching or practices of religious traditions, even though it seems easier to write about more general cultural traditions.

 Task

● Read again the marriage ceremony in **two** different religious traditions, and decide which you think are the most essential elements. Make a list of any practices that are common.

● Think about those elements that would make the day very special and memorable – what are they, and why do you think they make the day so special?

Q *Describe how people marry in **two** religious traditions* [6]

Look at the answer below. It has been given a Level 2 and 2 marks. What would you change or add to it, to give it a Level 4 and 6 marks?

Answer

Name of religious tradition: Christianity

How people marry: The two people fall in love and then become engaged. Once this engagement has taken place they go to church. They then register their names, and have a celebration meal, and maybe a party in the evening, before going off on their honeymoon.

Name of religious tradition: Islam

How people marry: The couple say prayers. The marriage is arranged by the two families, and often takes place in the mosque, or a large hall.

"My big thing
is I want to have
kids and a family."

(Robbie Williams,
pop star)

What about the children?

For many couples, an important part of getting married is the possibility of having children. This also means that couples will need to plan their family, and consider when to have children, and how many to have.

Christianity ✝

There are varying views about family planning within Christianity. Some Christians say that contraception is acceptable, provided that:

- Sex is within a marriage (or permanent relationship)
- Both partners agree to using contraception, and which kind to use.

This view is based on the belief that in family life, quality is the most important thing.

Others however, like some Roman Catholics, feel strongly that artificial methods of contraception are unacceptable. They would follow the rulings of the declaration of Pope Paul VI in *Humanae Vitae* that:

- Sexual intercourse should strengthen the bond between husband and wife
- Sexual intercourse should always be open to the possibility of creating new life.

As a result, they believe that couples should only use natural methods of family planning, such as the rhythm method, and that the sexual act is a total self-giving of two people to each other in love.

Yes. But the Bible does not have anything to say about contraception. Let's see, wasn't there something helpful in this book about general Christian principles?

OK, so we will use contraception for a while, and then have our children in a year or so. Is that all right with you?

Yes. Our children must be wanted as well as loved, and we can make sure we are ready and able to look after them too.

Hinduism

For some Hindus contraception is allowed, but for others it is considered as contrary to the practice of *ahimsa* (non-violence). Often social and economic factors are considered more influential than religious issues. Many couples do not believe that children should be conceived out of lust, and take part in the *garbhadhan samskara* when prayers are said to purify the womb and prepare the way for the soul of a new child to enter.

Islam

Attitudes to contraception may differ according to a couple's interpretation of Islamic tradition; however it should never be used to encourage promiscuity. Some couples do use artificial methods of contraception. Forms such as the pill and condom are generally considered more acceptable than those which are difficult to reverse, such as vasectomy.

Judaism

The procreation of children is believed to be part of the divine intention. In the book of Isaiah it states that when God made the world, 'he formed it to be inhabited' (Isaiah 45: 18).

Many Jews consider large families to be a blessing from God. There are a variety of opinions over whether it is acceptable to use contraceptives or not. Oral contraceptives are considered preferable to those forms of contraception which interfere with intercourse and where the male seed is destroyed. Condoms are generally considered as unacceptable as they prevent the true bonding of bodies.

Happily ever after?

Living with other people is not an easy thing, and being married to a person, and experiencing everything in life with that partner means that both people have to learn to give and take, and to work at making their relationship a happy and lasting one.

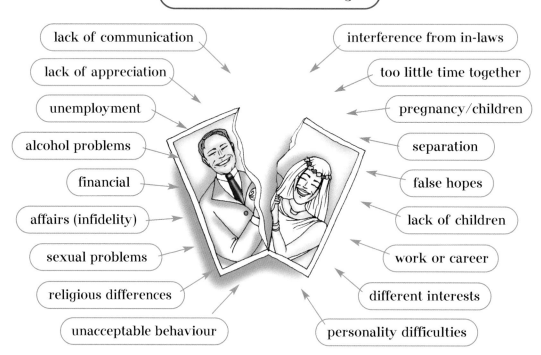

Pressures on Marriage

- lack of communication
- lack of appreciation
- unemployment
- alcohol problems
- financial
- affairs (infidelity)
- sexual problems
- religious differences
- unacceptable behaviour
- interference from in-laws
- too little time together
- pregnancy/children
- separation
- false hopes
- lack of children
- work or career
- different interests
- personality difficulties

Because of all these pressures, sometimes **conflict** comes into marriage and the family. When this happens, there needs to be some **reconciliation** if the couple and the family are to get along together, and build up their relationships.

 Task

- Can you think of other pressures on marriage?

- Choose 3 and say how you could help someone cope with them.

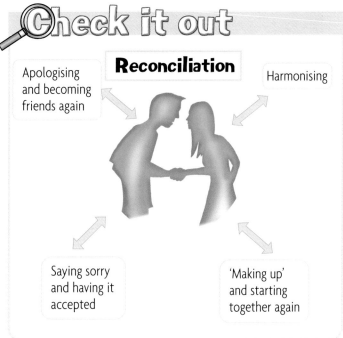

When things go wrong

What can religious communities do when things start to go wrong in a marriage?

- The religious leader can offer help and advice to the couple
- The community can offer marriage guidance counselling or therapy sessions
- Older and more experienced couples could talk with and support the couple having problems
- Family members could offer help and advice, especially in those religions where families have a specific role
- Prayers can be offered for or with the couple
- A group of 'young marrieds' could be run, to help discuss and share experiences and learning
- A pre-marriage course could be offered for all intending to get married
- A booklet or leaflet with religious teaching about marriage and family life could be prepared and given to couples when they marry.

Exam Tip

It is important when answering questions that ask for a point of view, that you express your thoughts clearly, and give reasons for what you think, with either good examples or illustrations, or specific religious teaching to support a view. Many candidates score low levels and marks because they just state a view without comment, explanation or justification. Also remember that you should *show that you have thought about more than one point of view*. So, acknowledge that there are other ideas, which also have reasons and justifications.

Q *'The best marriages are those where a couple fall in love with each other.' Do you agree? Give reasons or evidence for your answer, showing that you have thought about more than one point of view.* [6]

Look at the two answers below. Using the Levels of Response grids on page 117, decide what marks to give to each one. Then, choose one of them, and re-write it so that it gets full marks.

Answer A	Answer B
I do agree. I say this because falling in love first is a lot more practical, as you have got to know that person, and you both know how to keep one another happy. Of course there are some cultures and religions that arrange marriages, although it is expected that the couple will learn to love each other. Although such marriages can strengthen the bond of culture and ensure longevity, it is not the best for the people involved.	Some people would agree with the statement as if a couple are in love then it is more likely that they will stay together, as opposed to a couple who are forced together through an arranged marriage. Also, if a couple genuinely love each other, then it is more likely that they will be happy together and content with living together and sharing each other's company. They would also be more tolerant. In conclusion, I believe that the best marriages are those where a couple take time to get to know each other properly and develop a friendship as well as love, since friendships rarely fade, but love can fade. A close friendship would mean more tolerance of each other and marriage would mean a companionship and not just something to satisfy lust.

Point of no return

For many people, divorce is very much a last resort, when they have tried everything else, and still cannot make any reconciliation. Most religions have teachings about divorce and about re-marriage after divorce.

Christianity ✠

> **Is divorce acceptable?**

MAYBE

depending on individual circumstances

NO

It is not believed to be God's intention

It is a breaking of the solemn promises made before God and the Christian family

Anglicans:
- accept divorce, as UK law allows it;
- discourage re-marriage (but if chosen a non-church wedding is preferred); some ministers will agree to a service of prayer and dedication.

Non-conformists (E.g. Methodist/United Reformed)
- divorce best avoided;
- re-marriage permitted if it seems suitable or acceptable to all concerned;
- no minister can be forced to conduct a re-marriage ceremony against their will.

Roman Catholics:
- do not recognise divorce;
- marriage is a sacrament that cannot be dissolved except for special reasons (such as one partner not freely choosing to marry);
- some marriages can be annulled, where there are good reasons (such as the marriage never having been consummated).

Hinduism

> **Is divorce acceptable?**

SOMETIMES

As a last resort, or the sacramental concept of marriage would be meaningless.

Hindus of lower castes have always allowed divorce and the remarriage of both partners.

But it is uncommon because arranged marriages are less likely to break down.

The extended family would support a couple in their attempts to be reconciled.

Islam

Is divorce acceptable?

SOMETIMES

As a last resort. The Prophet Muhammad said: 'Of all the things which have been permitted divorce is the most hated by Allah.'

It is expected that the family will try to help the couple to be reconciled.

If the couple do decide to divorce then: The husband must state in front of witnesses on 3 separate occasions that the marriage is over.

A period of 3 months begins (*Iddah*). The couple will stay in the same house but not sleep together. *(This ensures that there is no confusion about who is the father of any children born after the divorce.)*

If the couple finally decide to divorce, then the wife is given the final part of her dowry. Both parties should act toward the other with kindness and charity.

Judaism

Is divorce acceptable?

❝ *When a man takes a wife and marries her, if then she finds no favour in his eyes because he has found some indecency in her, and he writes her a bill of divorce, and puts it in her hand ...* ❞

(Deuteronomy 24: 1–4)

YES **BUT ...**

It is always a last resort. The community will give support to try and keep the couple together.

A religious and a civil divorce must be obtained by all couples outside of Israel.

The couple will apply to the **Bet Din**, the religious court of rabbis, where the judges will question the witnesses and give their verdict.

In the Orthodox tradition the husband is expected to give a document of divorce (*get*) to the wife. This dissolves the marriage.

The divorce takes effect as soon as the woman receives the document.

The woman is allowed to remarry after 90 days.

Sometimes problems are caused where a husband has refused to give the woman a divorce, or where he cannot be traced; women in this situation are called *agunot* (chained).

See the picture about the 'Free the Agunot' campaign and prayer for Agunot on the next page.

Prayer for Agunot
(written by the International Coalition of Agunah Rights)

Creator of Heaven and Earth,
May it be your will to free the captive wives of Israel,
When love and sanctity have fled the home,
But their husbands bind them in the tatters of ketubot*.

Remove the bitter burden from these agunot
    and soften the hearts of their misguided captors.
Liberate your faithful daughters from their anguish.
Enable them to establish new homes and raise up
    children in peace.

Grant wisdom to the judges of Israel.
Teach them to recognise oppression and rule
    against it.
Infuse our rabbis with courage to use their power
    for good alone.
Blessed are you, Creator of heaven and earth,
    who frees the captives

[Baruch Mateir Asurim]

* wedding contracts

 Look it up http://members.aol.com/Agunah

TEST IT OUT

Here is a typical set of examination questions for this unit. Write out answers
to them, trying to take account of the Exam Tips and information you have been given.

(a) State **two** responsibilities married partners have to each other. [2]

(b) 'If they cannot exercise self control they should marry.
    For it is better to marry than to be aflame with passion.' (1 Corinthians 7: 9)
    Describe the main points of Christian teaching abut sex before marriage. [4]

(c) (i) What is 'adultery'? [2]
    (ii) Explain the teaching on adultery from **two** different religious traditions. [6]

(d) Explain how a religious family or community could help a couple if they begin to
    have problems in their marriage. (You may answer from any religious tradition.) [4]

(e) 'Couples who do not regularly take part in a religion should not be allowed to
    marry in a place of worship.' Do you agree? Give reasons or evidence for your
    answer, showing that you have thought about more than one point of view. [6]

3 Identity and belonging

How do people gain their identity?

Our identities are influenced by many different aspects:

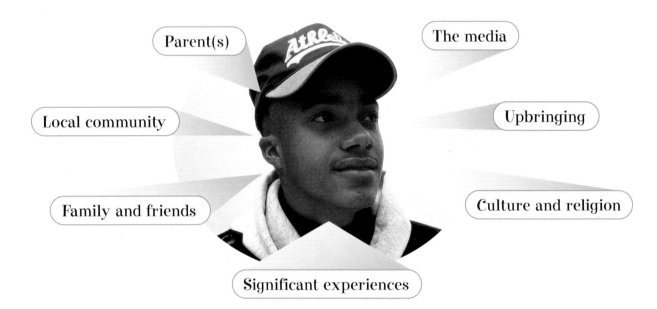

Parent(s)

The media

Local community

Upbringing

Family and friends

Culture and religion

Significant experiences

Check it out

Personality and character

Identity

One's own self

Condition of being a specified person

The way a person sees themselves

Task

- Can you think of other things that influence you as a person?

- What else makes you the person you are?

- What kind of authorities affect your choices in life? (You can refer to page 93 for 'Check it out' on Authority.)

Welcome

All religions consider it important to thank God as they welcome a baby into the world. Many religions have a special ceremony that marks the entrance of a baby into the community of believers.

Check it out

A company of people

Community

A religious 'family' or group

A group of people with something in common

A fellowship of people

As we have seen in Chapter Two, the birth of a baby is a very special event. Religions teach about the **sanctity of life**, and therefore the birth of a baby is really special. To celebrate this special relationship, and to thank God, most religions hold a ceremony which marks the baby's entrance into the religious community. Sometimes, within a religious tradition, what happens in these ceremonies, may differ as families decide their own preferences.

> **SANCTITY OF LIFE –** the belief that all life is sacred and unique

Christianity ✝

Usually a baby will be welcomed into the Christian Church a few months after its birth. As a baby cannot speak for itself, the parents and god-parents in an Anglican or Roman Catholic baptism make certain promises; these promises may be confirmed by the child when older. It is believed God grants the child salvation through baptism. For all Christian traditions it is a symbol of a new beginning. Each child is considered a gift from God, and children are expected to honour their parents, as a duty to God (Exodus 20: 12).

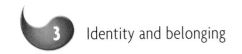

Admission — Entry to the Christian Church is marked by this ceremony, which usually occurs on a Sunday so the church community can be present.

Naming — The baby's name is usually announced, or given; sometimes it is referred to as a 'Christian' name.

God-parents — The ceremony will usually include god-parents – who are to ensure the child will grow spiritually – along with the parents, other family members and the congregation.

Light candle — A lighted candle is often given to the parents and god-parents to show they have made special promises.

Intentions — The promises made declare the parents', god-parents', and congregation's intentions to help the child fight against evil and so pass from darkness to light.

Confirmed — As the child becomes older, some believe that they should take part in a special service of confirmation. This is a service which confirms the promises and intentions made for them by their parents and god-parents.

Adults — The *confirmation* service allows the 'children' to become adult members of the church. This is such an important ceremony that the bishop will lay hands on each person, believing that the power of the Holy Spirit is passed on to them.

Nurture — The expectation is that, following baptism, the child will be brought up – or nurtured – in the Christian way of life.

Community — The god-parents represent the community, and the minister represents the church, in this welcome ceremony.

Admission — Entry to the Christian church and community is gained through the baptism ceremony.

Transform — The pouring of water on the baby's head is a sign of new spiritual life; through the forgiveness of sin and the presence of the Holy Spirit, the child's life is being transformed, or changed.

Holy Spirit — Chrism is rubbed onto the baby's forehead to show the Holy Spirit is given to the child. (Chrism is an aromatic oil, blessed during Easter week).

Original sin — It is believed everyone is born with sin, or the ability to sin, in them. This is called 'original sin', and it is the baptism that is cleansing this sin away.

Light candle — A lighted candle is given as a symbol of Jesus Christ – the Light of the World.

Intentions — Parents and god-parents promise to make sure that the child is brought up in the Christian tradition.

Communicant — After baptism, the child will take part in mass, and so are communicant members of the congregation. As they become older they will also go for confirmation.

Baptists

Baptist Churches do not practise the baptising of babies or young
children. They believe that baptism should be for adults, or at
least children who are able to understand the importance of what
they are doing. This ceremony is sometimes called 'Believers' Baptism'.
Many Baptist churches also have a Dedication ceremony for babies,
when the parents bring the child to a Sunday service, and give thanks
to God for the child, and 'dedicate' the child to God, promising to
bring it up in the Christian way of life.

Believers	The ceremony is for those who believe for themselves, and who freely choose to be baptised.
Adult	It is an acknowledgement of being able to understand what you are doing, and that you are obeying the command of Christ to be baptised.
Public	The ceremony is always performed in the presence of the congregation. It is a public declaration of personal faith and commitment.
Testimony	Candidates for baptism usually give their own spoken testimony, or give answers to a series of questions that demonstrate their faith.
Immersion	The person is immersed in the water, and this symbolises the dying to sin (the body is 'buried'). Being lifted up out of the water again is to signify the rising to new life (the body is 'resurrected')
Sins	The water also symbolises the washing away of sins, and the accepting of the forgiveness of them through faith in Jesus.
Teaching	Usually, before baptism, candidates will be taught the meanings of the ceremony, and the importance of living the Christian life. As they grow in their faith, they would be expected to participate fully in the life of the church.

Roman Catholic baptism

Anglican baptism

Baptism
by immersion

Hinduism ॐ

When a new baby is born, there will usually be much happiness. It is believed that the baby's soul will carry with it the good and bad deeds from the past life.

Havan	A fire (*havan*) is lit and offerings of ghee and grams are made. A long life is wished for the baby. Often the *aum* (sacred symbol) will be traced onto the baby's tongue with something sweet.
Impurities	The child is washed after its birth to cleanse any impurities from a past life.
Naming	A ceremony of naming will happen ten to twelve days after birth (*nam samskara*). The baby is washed and dressed in new clothes, and prayers are said. Offerings of flowers and fruit are made at shrines of the deities in the temple.
Date	The exact date and time of birth are located so the priest can work out the baby's horoscope. Using this information the priest will work out the first letter of the baby's name.
Upanayana	Some boys who belong to the first three castes will have an *upanayana* (sacred thread) ceremony later on.
Initiation	The upanayana ceremony is an initiation and is performed in front of family and friends, and during it the boy will make a vow to remain celibate until he is married, and to fulfil his duties to God, his parents and his religious teacher.
Samskaras	There are 16 samskaras or stages of life in Hinduism. The first three take place before birth. The 4th and 5th are the tracing of the aum and the naming ceremonies, and upanayana is the 10th.
Mundan	This is the name given to the first cutting of hair, when the baby is around the age of one year. It is believed by Hindus that this ceremony is a way of making any impurities from past lives be washed away. At this ceremony parents hope that the child will be blessed with a fresh start in this new life.

Celebrating one of the samskaras

Islam ☾★

Each child is considered a gift from Allah. There are certain rituals that begin as soon as the baby is born. As the baby grows, he or she will be expected to – *'show kindness to your parents. If one of them or both of them grow old with you, do not say a word of contempt to them or rebuke them, but speak respectfully to them. Lower the wing of humility to them through mercy, and say, "My Lord, have mercy on them, as they raised me up when I was little".'*
(Surah 17: 23–4)

Ist	The first word a baby hears will be that of Allah, as the *adhan* (call to prayer) is whispered in the baby's ear, as soon as possible after birth.
Seventh	On the seventh day after birth, there is the cutting of the baby's hair (*aqiqah*). Offerings of charity to thank Allah for the gift of the child are made, usually gold or silver equivalent to the weight of the hair shaved, is given to the poor.
Longing	Little sweet objects, such as sugar or honey are put onto the baby's gum. This is called *taneek*, and symbolises the longing, or hope that the baby's life will be sweet.
Allah	Allah commanded Ibrahim to circumcise the males in his household. This is observed in the *khitan* ceremony where boys are circumcised; this usually happens up to the age of ten years.
Madrassah	As the child grows they will probably attend the mosque school, or *madrassah*. Often there is a family party when a child has learnt the Arabic alphabet, and can recite a few surahs of the Qur'an. This is called the *Bismillah* ceremony, and marks the early stages of learning the Muslim way of life.

After *aqiqah*

Learning at a *madrassah*

Judaism

The type of celebrations that the baby will have will depend on whether the baby is born into an Orthodox or Reform branch of Judaism. As children grow they are expected to fulfil certain duties to their parents. (Exodus 20: 12)

Jews	Jews and God have a special bond, which is through the covenant of circumcision.
Eight	Eight days after the birth of a Jewish boy, the *Brit Milah* (circumcision) is held to reflect the belief that God commanded Abraham to circumcise the males in the household.
Watched	Only males are allowed to watch the circumcision, which is performed by a *mohel* on behalf of the father. The *mohel* is licensed by the Bet Din.
Initiation	As Brit Milah symbolises entering into the covenantal relationship, so it will be expected that the child will be initiated into the adult congregation, through the *Bar Mitzvah* (son of the commandment) ceremony, usually at the age of 13 years. This ceremony signifies that the boy is responsible to keep the laws in the Torah, wear the *tallit* (prayer shawl), and keep fasts such as *Yom Kippur*. (Girls may have a *Bat Mitzvah* or a *Bat Chayil* ceremony) *
Sandek	The godfather is known as *sandek*, and the baby is laid on a cushion on the sandek's knees. Here, the mohel carries out the circumcision.
Hebrew	As the child becomes older they will often start to attend *cheder* (synagogue religion classes). Here they will learn the Hebrew language, and learn more about the Jewish festivals.

* Depending on which branch of Judaism they belong to: girls may choose to have a Bat Mitzvah (daughter of the commandment) if they are in the Reform Movement; girls in the Orthodox tradition may choose to the Bat Chayil ceremony (daughter of worth). These are often near the girls' 12th birthday.

Preparation for Bat Chayil at a cheder

The Bar Mitzvah ceremony

Why festivals and celebrations?

Why do religions have festivals and celebrations? What do believers gain from them?

These two questions are central to this unit. Generally, across most religions, the following reasons or benefits would be claimed:

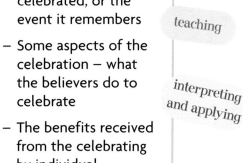

historical origins   *important people*   *strenthening*

- remembering important events in the **history** of the religion
- commemorating events in the lives of **important people** in the religion
- **confirming** faith, **strengthening** belief
- **teaching** the young of the community, and developing their faith
- increase or develop the **sense of community** and identity
- **interpreting and applying** beliefs or doctrines to everyday life
- acknowledging the **world-wide** aspect of religion
- **witnessing** to others outside the faith
- **celebrating** the good and positive things in life

conforming   *teaching*   *interpreting and applying*   *witnessing*

sense of community   *worldwide*   *celebrating*

But festivals and celebrations, by their nature, are events in which individuals in the community are involved. The benefits described above can only be gained when a person actively participates in the event and is affected by the experience.

Task

- From the two or three religions you are studying, select a number of festivals, and make a chart that will help you remember the following things about them:
  - The name of the festival, and which religion
  - The reason it is celebrated, or the event it remembers
  - Some aspects of the celebration – what the believers do to celebrate
  - The benefits received from the celebrating by individual believers and or the religious community as a whole.

Exam Tip

Always make sure you are specific when talking about the significance or meaning of festivals and celebrations. Try to recall only the key elements and the important aspects; remember the underlying focus of this unit is how festivals and celebrations **show identity and belonging**.

Check it out

A ceremony to mark an event

A religious festival or event

Celebration

A service or ritual enacted according to tradition

A special occasion

A religious ceremony that takes place regularly

Worship and celebration

Celebrating festivals is an important part of any religion. Most religions have a variety of festivals, but only one or two are shown in the collages that follow. You will be able to use websites(*) and other resources to find out further information.

* a useful website can be found at the foot of each page.

Christianity ✞

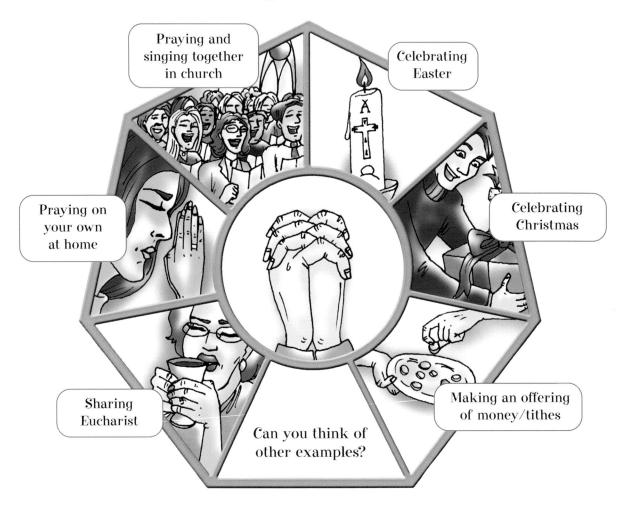

Praying and singing together in church

Celebrating Easter

Praying on your own at home

Celebrating Christmas

Sharing Eucharist

Making an offering of money/tithes

Can you think of other examples?

Task

- Select any aspect of worship and celebration in Christianity. Explain how it helps people express and affirm their identity as Christians.

REMEMBER
You should be able to write about two or three festivals or celebrations from each of the religions you study.

 Look it up http://www.jcrerlations.net/australia/ccjiv/festivals2.htm

Hinduism ॐ

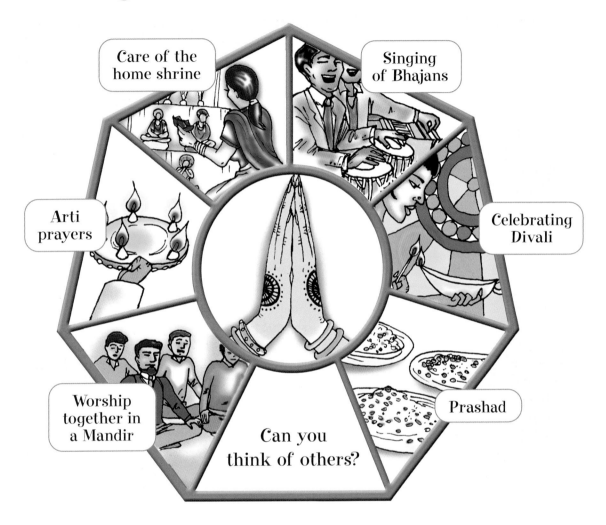

Care of the home shrine

Singing of Bhajans

Arti prayers

Celebrating Divali

Worship together in a Mandir

Prashad

Can you think of others?

Task

- Select any aspect of worship and celebration in Hinduism. Explain how it helps people express and affirm their identity as Hindus.

REMEMBER
You should be able to write about two or three festivals or celebrations from each of the religions you study.

Look it up http://www.iskcon.net/ies/festival.html

Islam

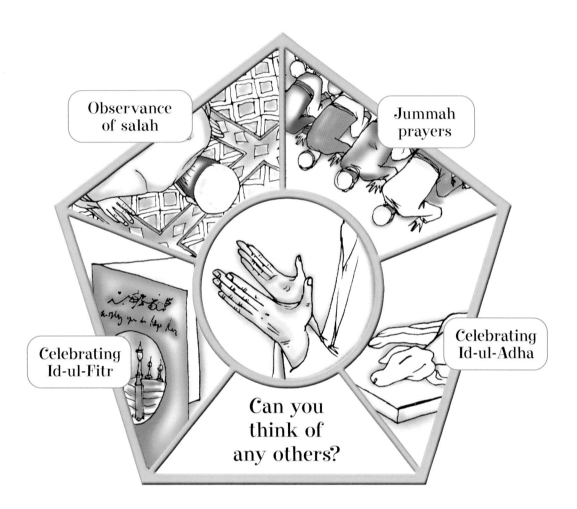

Observance of salah

Jummah prayers

Celebrating Id-ul-Fitr

Celebrating Id-ul-Adha

Can you think of any others?

• Select any aspect of worship and celebration in Islam. Explain how it helps people express and affirm their identity as Muslims.

REMEMBER
You should be able to write about two or three festivals or celebrations from each of the religions you study.

 Look it up http://www.mrc.org.uk/festivals.htm

Judaism

Blessing

Worshipping together in synagogue

Worshipping alone

Keeping Shabbat

Celebrating Pesach

Reading Sefer Torah

Can you think of other examples?

Observing Yom Kippur

Task

- Select any aspect of worship and celebration in Judaism. Explain how it helps people express and affirm their identity as Jews.

REMEMBER
You should be able to write about two or three festivals or celebrations from each of the religions you study.

Look it up http://www.melizo.com/festivals

57

Symbols of belonging

Many people wear or use symbols to represent their commitment to a particular religious or cultural tradition.

The symbols that follow are stated in the Specification, but you will be able to find many more.

Christianity ✝

Fish sign

'I like to wear a **fish sign**: it reminds me of Jesus, and also tells other people that I am a Christian. It is a symbol used in the times of the persecution of Christians, and came from the Greek word for fish (*icthus*) which makes up a useful summary of my beliefs: Jesus Christ, God's Son, Saviour.'

Crucifix

'My gran gave me my **crucifix** after my confirmation. I always wear it round my neck on a chain. It helps me, especially when I'm worried or upset, and I remember that God is with me wherever I go.'

Vestments

'These **vestments** help to show that the ceremony is a special and important one; it makes me feel humble to be part of such a long tradition; and privileged to be able to lead the ceremony. It is not obligatory to wear them, but I think it helps make Communion holy.'

Salvationist uniform

'Our **uniform** speaks of order and discipline, and reminds everyone what we stand for: war against evil and suffering; fighting for God and salvation. I am proud to wear it because I am proud of my faith, and of the God I serve.'

Hinduism

Aum symbol

'The **aum** is the most sacred of Hindu words. It is believed to be the first sound ever uttered. When my brother was born the aum was traced onto his tongue with honey. I have an incense holder with the aum symbol on it.'

Swastika

'The **swastika** is a symbol we use for good fortune. It can often be found on Divali cards or on rangoli patterns. The four arms represent the four directions, the four Vedas and the four stages in the life cycle. It really upsets me when people think it is the symbol for Nazis. It was around centuries before them.'

Tilak mark

'Originally a tilak would be made on the forehead with ash or sandalwood paste but now they can be bought in packs to stick on. My mum wears hers to show she's married, but when I'm going somewhere special then I wear one.'

Islam

Dress

'I decided to wear **hijab** as soon as I started secondary school. It may appear as just a head-scarf but it means so much more to me. It tells me in the Qur'an that it is a way of keeping purity and helps people to see me as I really am – not as a sex symbol. My mother wears the **chador** – this is the black veil to cover almost all her face apart from, her eyes. When she was young in Iran, she started to wear it and now she feels uncomfortable if she goes outside without it on. I know she is proud of her chador like I am of my hijab. We both feel it is a part of our religion and identity.'

Star and crescent

'When I am abroad I always look to see where a mosque may be. Usually I can spot one by a star and crescent being on top of the building. These symbols are important because it is a reminder that Islam guides and lights the way through life, just as the star and moon do in the night.'

Judaism

Kippah

'If someone sees my dad and I in the street they can tell right away that we are Jewish because we both wear a **kippah**. When I put it on in the morning I feel that it straight away shows my respect to God by covering that part of my body which is nearest to Him. The colour doesn't matter – at school I wear one the same colour as the school uniform.'

Tallit

'My **tallit** was given to me for my Bar Mitzvah, and I know that when I get older I would like to pass it down to my sons, although I know my grandfather was wrapped in his when he was buried. I wear it every morning at prayers. The fringes help remind me of the 613 *mitzvot* or duties which are mentioned in the Torah and are part of the relationship or covenant with God. My sister is of the Liberal Jewish tradition and she has now decided that she too wants to show her religious identity by wearing a kippah and tallit.'

Tefillin

'It took me a while until I could learn to lay **tefillin** properly. These are leather boxes which are tied to the head and upper arm during morning prayers and contain important passages from the Torah. They remind me that I need to serve God with my head and my heart. I feel proud when I wear them because as well as reinforcing my identity as an Orthodox Jew I know I am keeping the duty described in Deuteronomy 6: 8.'

Star of David

'I wear my **Star of David**, or **Magen David**, all the time around my neck. It is not a religious duty to wear it, but I feel it is a mark of my identity as the symbol is often connected with Judaism. Nobody knows how it became one, but now you see the symbol on many synagogues, on the Israeli flag, and on greetings cards for Jewish festivals amongst other things.'

> **Q** *Describe and explain **two** different religious symbols of belonging. You may choose from either **ONE** or **TWO** religious traditions.* [6]

Look at the example below. The candidate has tried to answer the question carefully. Using the Levels of Response Grids on page 117, decide what Level and mark you think it is worth.

Answer

(i) Name of religious tradition: Christianity

Symbol of belonging: A cross is two pieces of wood or metal arranged in the form of a plus sign, although the down piece is longer. A crucifix has a model of the body of Jesus on it. Either may be worn as a necklace, or a pin-badge, and shows that the wearer belongs to the Christian faith. It reminds them of what Jesus, the Son of God, did for them, and shows their faith. It also tells other people that they follow the teachings of Jesus.

(ii) Name of religious tradition: Islam

Symbol of belonging: The ihram is a special cloth worn by Muslim pilgrims. It shows that they are on pilgrimage to Makkah, and that they are Muslims. Pilgrimage is a very important part of Islam. All Muslims are expected to go on pilgrimage at least once in their lifetime.

The last two sentences, whilst being correct in themselves, do not actually add anything to answer the question being asked.

Exam Tip

This unit is all about identity and belonging, and so it is important to remember that answers to questions about festivals and celebrations, or about symbols used by believers, will need to refer to how they **show identity and belonging**. Make sure you read the question carefully, and look out for the key words – do not just write everything you can remember about a festival or a symbol of belonging.

A description is given, as referred to in the question

There are clear ideas of identity and belonging stated.

A correct technical term is used; but there is no description of the ihram.

There is reference to identity and belonging – but more could be added.

Task

- Use the pointers above to help you decide on the Level and mark, and to re-write the answer to gain full marks.

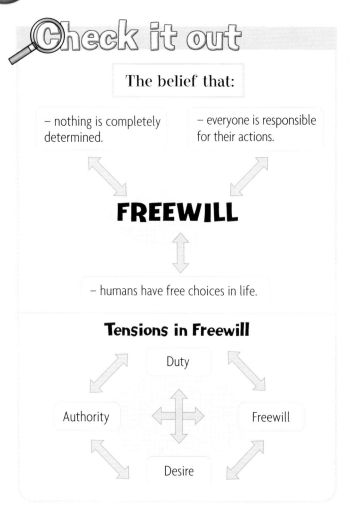

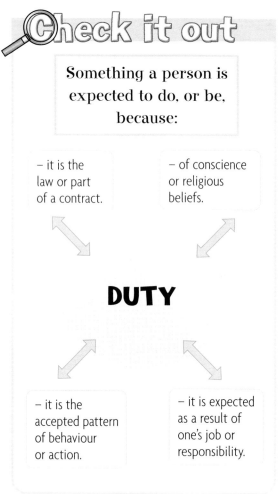

The question about whether or not humans have free will is often talked and written about. Some religions have clear views and beliefs about the matter, and within religious traditions there are varying opinions too. You will come across more of this issue in Chapter 4, Looking for Meaning, but here are some of the ideas involved:

- humans were created with free will;
- for any action to be truly 'human' it must come from a conscious and free choice;
- if human beings do not have free will, then they can not be held responsible for their actions;
- human nature has a flaw and potential weakness, which affects the way we choose;
- beliefs and values, which may be matters of choice, do influence behaviour;
- inherited personality traits, experience, and selfish interests also influence behaviour, and perhaps beliefs and attitudes;
- not all people's religion or culture is their own free choice, and no one has the choice of where and to whom they are born;
- where religion or way of life is a deliberate personal choice, there often follows a path of duty and the need for obedience or submission;

● where choices are freely made, the outcomes resulting from them have a direct impact on our experience.

The issue is complex and difficult, but thinking about and discussing the issues above will help you sort out your own thinking.

Look at the following errors that have been found in past papers.

Can you work out what the candidates were writing about?

Can you give the correct term?

Naming religions:		Technical terms:	
'Believers'	'Christian Aid'	'rights of passage'	'chowdor'
'Jewdaists'	'Reincarnationists'	'christianising'	'Ucharist'
'Jewdaists'	'atheists'	'conformation'	'cruscificks'
'Islamics'		'moal'	

Try to be accurate with names of religions and technical terms; you will not gain full credit for answers to questions otherwise.

● Make a chart of the religions you are studying, and note down all the technical terms and proper names you ought to remember. Learn their spellings and meanings carefully.

Exam Tip

Many candidates lose marks because they do not use technical terms correctly, and do not even give the proper name for the religious traditions they are writing about. Although marks are not taken off for these inaccuracies, it is not possible to gain full marks if they are incorrect.

TEST IT OUT

Here is a typical set of examination questions for this unit. Write out answers to them, trying to take account of the Exam Tips and information you have been given.

(a) State **three** things that affect a person's identity or character. [3]

(b) (i) Name **one** rite of passage from a religious tradition. [1]
    (ii) Explain how that rite of passage is important in showing a person's belonging to the faith community. [4]

(c) (i) State **two** benefits believers may get from worshipping or praying on their own. [2]
    (ii) State **two** benefits believers may get from worshipping, praying or celebrating with others in a public place of worship. [2]

(d) Explain why **two** religious festivals are important in the religion.
(You may choose your two examples from just one religion, **or** you may give one example from each of two religious traditions.) [6]

(e) 'Duty rules out free will'. Do you agree? Give reasons or evidence for your answer, showing that you have thought about more than one point of view. [6]

4 God, life & death

What is God like?

Unfortunately there is nobody here to answer your question at the moment, but if you would care to leave a message after the pip ...

Check it out

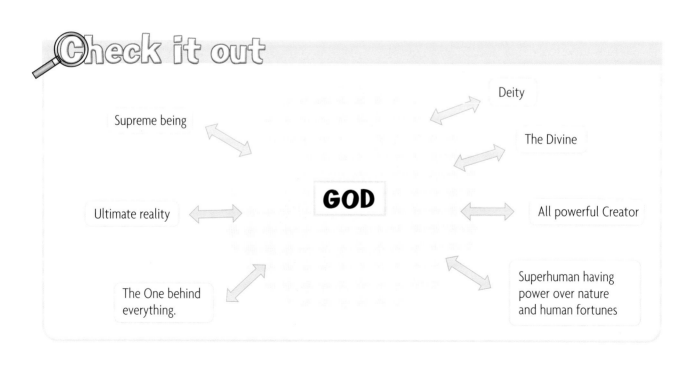

Supreme being ←→ GOD ←→ Deity

The Divine

Ultimate reality ←→ GOD ←→ All powerful Creator

The One behind everything.

Superhuman having power over nature and human fortunes

The nature of God

Many people wonder at some time in their life whether or not there is a God or supreme being, and also what they might be like. Views often include:

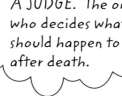

A GREAT ARCHITECT! The designer of the world.

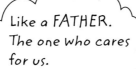

A JUDGE. The one who decides what should happen to us after death.

A She, not a He!!

I cannot believe that there has never been a God, an omniscient being who knows everything.

Like a FATHER. The one who cares for us.

I believe God is omnipotent, who has power over all creation.

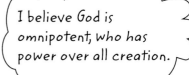

People's views on the nature of God are often influenced by a range of things:

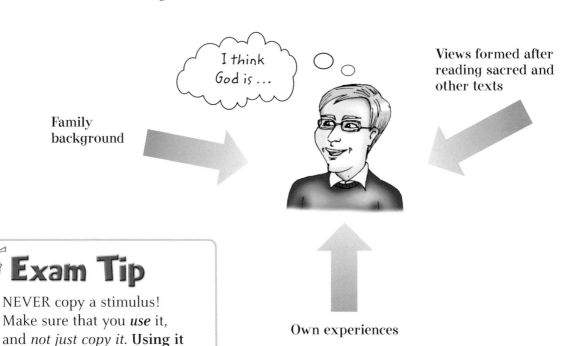

I think God is ...

Family background

Views formed after reading sacred and other texts

Own experiences

Exam Tip

NEVER copy a stimulus! Make sure that you *use* it, and *not just copy it*. **Using it** means explaining what the stimulus is and how it answers the question being asked.

Q *Describe two things that influence people's ideas about God?* [4]

[The stimulus for this question is the diagram above]

Look at the answer below. It would not gain any marks at all. Can you say why? Amend the answer so that it is worth the full marks for this question.

Answer
(i) Family background (ii) Own experiences

Check it out

Symbolism

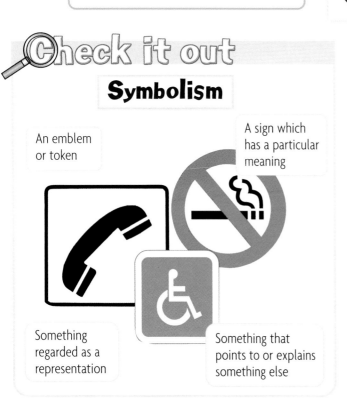

An emblem or token

A sign which has a particular meaning

Something regarded as a representation

Something that points to or explains something else

Symbolism and imagery

Within many religions believers will possess or wear certain objects that they consider have a deeper meaning or help them express their belief in God. Often these symbols are considered sacred by the believers and can be used to aid worship.

Christianity

The Cross

Christians believe that Jesus is the best way that people can know about God. So the cross, which is a reminder of the death and resurrection of Jesus, is a helpful reminder of beliefs in God and his character.

Christians believe that God is One, but is known or experienced through three distinct persons: Father, Son and Holy Spirit. They call this 'The Trinity'.

Christians do not pretend that this belief is easy to understand or explain, but many different examples are used to help understanding.

'Water' is one of the most common ideas used to explain Trinity. The chemical formula for water is H_2O, but as water it is in liquid form. H_2O is also a solid – which we call ice; and also a gas or vapour – which we call steam. Ice, steam and water are very different things – but each is still H_2O.

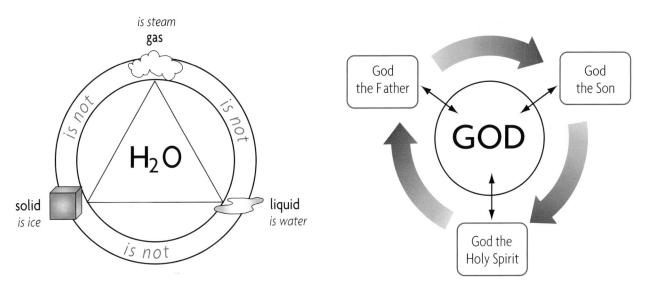

So with the Trinity, although there are three 'persons', the three are God-as-one. Each 'person' is an aspect of God's nature which humans are able to perceive and begin to understand.

In this way, Christians believe that God is Three-in-One. But the most complete revelation of God, say Christians, is through Jesus Christ. They believe him to be God's Son, born of the Virgin Mary, and yet also a human being – 'God in the flesh'. This was how he was able to 'reveal' to people something of God's true nature.

God loved the world so much that he gave his only Son so that whoever believes in him may not be lost, but have eternal life..

[John 3: 16]

Christians believe that Jesus' death on the cross was the greatest act of love, as he gave himself up to die for all people. His resurrection on Easter Sunday was the overcoming of sin and death, so bringing new life and hope to the world.

As such, Christians call Jesus:

Meaning –
- he is equal with God, his father
- he is ruler of the world and of heaven
- the One who directs or guides a believer's life.

→ **Lord**

And also:

Redeemer ←

Meaning –
- the One who pays the ransom price to set others free
- the bringer of forgiveness
- the One who gives eternal life.

There are also many other titles for Jesus. You might like to try and find out what some of them are, and what they mean.

Exam Tip

You must give *accurate* descriptions, explanations and spellings of key words and concepts. They are listed in the specification, so learn them.

 Q *Christians describe Jesus as 'Lord' and 'Redeemer'. Explain the meaning of **each** of these titles.* [4]

Look at the four answers below. One was given 4 marks, and another 2 marks. Can you work out which two of the four, and why?

Answer A
Jesus as 'Lord' means: Mightier than anyone and the most powerful. Jesus as 'Redeemer' means: He is merciful and will 'Redeem' any problems.

Answer C
Jesus as 'Lord' means: God made Jesus as his son so people see him as holy. Jesus as 'Redeemer' means: Because he is holy he is worshipped.

Answer B
Jesus as 'Lord' means: Jesus is seen as God because of the Trinity: Jesus, Father, God. Jesus as 'Redeemer' means: Redeemer of humans.

Answer D
Jesus as 'Lord' means: He is someone we should worship, he is higher than us and perfect, and we should live our lives through his teachings. Jesus as 'Redeemer' means: He died on the cross and redeemed his followers. He took away their sin and forgave them, cleansing them of 'original sin'.

 **Look it up** http://www-cyweb.com/~dschmidt/qv-docs/qv-pap/jesunam.htm

Hinduism ॐ

Murti

Hindus believe that Brahman is everywhere, the real self in all beings, and the Supreme Spirit.

Murtis are images of the deities on whom the devotion is focused. Most Hindus will have murtis of their own *Ishta-dev* (chosen deity) in their home shrine.

The *trimurti* is represented by Brahma – the creator; Vishnu – the preserver; and Shiva – the destroyer. So reflecting the pattern of birth, growth and death that the world is constantly going through.

Using murti in devotion

Islam ☪

The Wise

The Creator

The Most Merciful

The Subhah

The One who gives peace

The Friend

Muslims believe in the One God, Allah, from whom all things were created. The belief in the unity of Allah is called *tawhid*. In the revelation of the Qur'an, Allah is given 99 attributes or names. Many Muslims use a *subhah* which is a string of 99 beads. Each bead represents one of the qualities of Allah. Many Muslims use the beads daily as an aid to worship.

Eternal

The Light

Using a subhah

The One who gives life

The One who gives death

The Protector

69

Judaism

The Mezuzah

The belief in the oneness of God in Judaism is found in the Shema which is recited by many Jews in the evening and morning services. The first paragraph comes from Deuteronomy 6 v 4-9, and states:

> Hear, O Israel: the Lord our God is one Lord, and you shall love the Lord your God with all your heart, and with all your soul, and with all your might. And these words I command you this day shall be upon your heart; and you shall teach them diligently to your children, and shall talk of them when you sit in your house, and when you walk by the way, and when you lie down, and when you rise. And you shall bind them as a sign upon your hand, and they shall be as frontlets between your eyes. And you shall write them on the doorposts of your house and on your gates.

Many Jewish homes have a *mezuzah* case on their front door. In the case are the first two verses of the Shema. It is also rolled into *tefillin* boxes which are strapped onto the forehead and arms and head and neck for morning prayers on weekdays.

Wearing tefillin

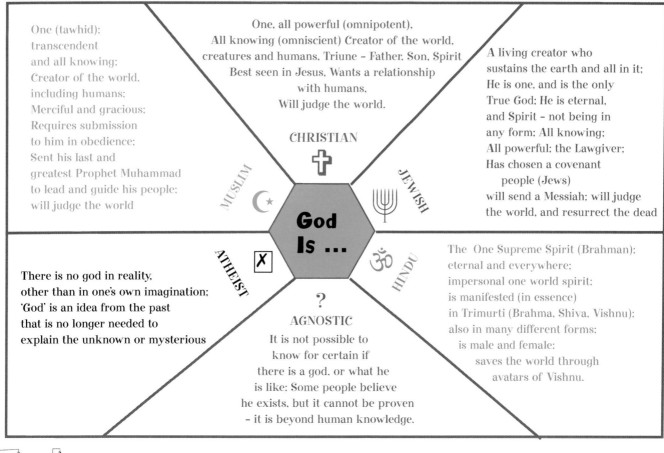

One (tawhid):
transcendent
and all knowing:
Creator of the world,
including humans:
Merciful and gracious:
Requires submission
to him in obedience:
Sent his last and
greatest Prophet Muhammad
to lead and guide his people:
will judge the world

One, all powerful (omnipotent),
All knowing (omniscient) Creator of the world,
creatures and humans, Triune - Father, Son, Spirit
Best seen in Jesus, Wants a relationship
with humans,
Will judge the world.

CHRISTIAN

MUSLIM

JEWISH

God Is ...

A living creator who
sustains the earth and all in it:
He is one, and is the only
True God: He is eternal,
and Spirit - not being in
any form: All knowing:
All powerful: the Lawgiver:
Has chosen a covenant
    people (Jews)
will send a Messiah: will judge
the world, and resurrect the dead

ATHEIST

HINDU

There is no god in reality,
other than in one's own imagination:
'God' is an idea from the past
that is no longer needed to
explain the unknown or mysterious

?

AGNOSTIC

It is not possible to
know for certain if
there is a god, or what he
is like: Some people believe
he exists, but it cannot be proven
- it is beyond human knowledge.

The One Supreme Spirit (Brahman):
eternal and everywhere:
impersonal one world spirit:
is manifested (in essence)
in Trimurti (Brahma, Shiva, Vishnu):
also in many different forms:
    is male and female:
        saves the world through
            avatars of Vishnu.

Task

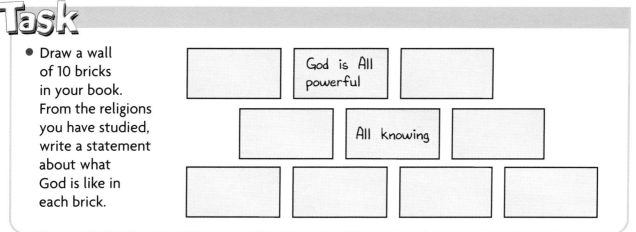

- Draw a wall of 10 bricks in your book. From the religions you have studied, write a statement about what God is like in each brick.

God is All powerful

All knowing

Why do people believe in God?

For many people their views about God change. This might depend on their experiences, age, and friends.

Many people will change their views between faith, and doubt.

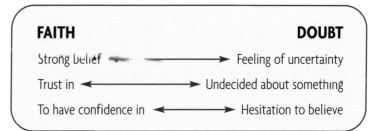

FAITH		DOUBT
Strong belief	← →	Feeling of uncertainty
Trust in	← →	Undecided about something
To have confidence in	← →	Hesitation to believe

Check it out

Agnostic

cannot be known

A person who believes it is not possible to know whether or not God exists

Someone who feels that proof of God is beyond human knowledge

A person who is not sure if you can know if there is such a thing as God

Check it out

Atheist

No God

A person who believes there is no God

A person who is convinced that God is not real

Someone who is sure that ideas of God are imagined

Someone who believes there is no need to believe in God

Exam Tip

When giving a definition, do not confuse the meanings of related terms. Candidates often lose marks this way. You need to learn the key concepts.

The most recent survey shows that there has been an increase in the number of people who do not believe in God.

Q (i) What is an atheist? [2]
(ii) What is an agnostic? [2]

Look at the answer below? Do you think it should have full marks for both parts? Explain your reasons.

Answer

(i) An atheist is a person that carries no religious beliefs. They believe that there is no higher power.

(ii) An agnostic is someone who is not sure about religion and does not know what to believe.

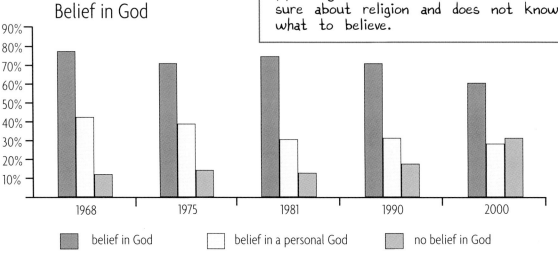

Belief in God

(*The Tablet*, 3 June, 2000)

How do people experience God?

A miracle

Act of benevolence

Worship

Prayer

An inner feeling

Reading Sacred texts

Natural beauty and wonder

Miracle

A miracle is usually regarded as something that is a wonder, a supernatural happening; something that wouldn't happen in the normal ordinary course of events.

For many people, in different religions, something that happens because of prayer, or faith that is 'miraculous' is an experience of God, and a sense of his reality and presence.

> This story is set in Zimbabwe before it became independent, during times of intense guerrilla warfare. People on farms owned by 'whites' were not safe, and great security was necessary.

On arriving at her parents' farm in a dangerous area of Salisbury, Elspeth discovered to her dismay that her parents had gone away for the night. She felt afraid but busied herself with chores until it grew dark. Just as darkness fell she found to her horror that she had left her washing outside on the line. It was dangerous to leave it out all night as it would let any wandering guerrillas think the farm was deserted, but it was even more dangerous to go out into the darkness. What should she do? She prayed for help and direction and God gave her a very clear thought: 'Go out and get the washing in as quickly as possible and keep praying all the time.

She did this and got back inside without incident. The night passed peacefully, but next morning a security patrol arrived and asked anxiously if she was safe. Was she disturbed during the night? When she said she had not been, they appeared amazed. 'Then who was with you last night?' they asked. She replied that she had been quite alone. The officer then told her that they had captured some guerrillas who said they had been about to attack her home after dark the previous night and were watching from nearby bushland. Then they had seen her come out to take the washing and with her was an armed man, and the whole scene was brilliantly lit. She had been conversing with him all the while.

(from 'Guardian Angel' in *A Hand on My Shoulder* by N. Cook & V. Frampton)

Act of Benevolence

Sometimes a miracle is experienced almost as if it were an act of generosity by God, like the grandfather who went on pilgrimage to Makkah, and escaped from a raging fire that tore through the tents in Mina.

Worship

For many religious people they feel they have a direct relationship and communication with God through their worship.

Prayer

For many people, prayer is something very real. It is a way of thinking about God, and feeling that life is different as a result of praying. Take the example of actor Paul J. Medford, who says: '*When I get in, I check my e-mails and often phone my mum in Barbados, because the time difference is right for her then. I pray in bed. I'm not deeply religious, but I believe that God makes all things possible.*'

An Inner Feeling

Sometimes people just feel that God is there, helping them and supporting them, even when things are not appearing too good. The singer Gloria Gaynor explains: '*I'd quit singing because I'd become a born-again Christian and I wanted to know for certain what God wanted me to do with my life. … I had no income, but during that time I wasn't concerned where the next meal was coming from, but I believed God would supply my needs, and he did.*'

Reading Sacred Texts

Many religious people find sacred texts have a special meaning for them at a particular time and moment in their life. As they read, they feel moved and inspired, and sometimes that the words were much more than just words on a page; but as if God were 'speaking' to them directly.

Yusuf Islam said, after reading a copy of the Qu'ran, 'A feeling of belonging ran through me. I was a stream that had found its ocean.'

Natural beauty and wonder

There are many beautiful things in the world of nature – and sometimes a person feels a sense of awareness that there is a God involved in it all, somewhere.

How do people respond to God?

Prayer

Prayer is a regular feature of many peoples' lives. Sometimes people pray together or on their own. In many religions there are particular times or patterns of praying that believers follow.

Preaching and teaching

Sharing the faith with others, and helping each other to grow in faith is an aspect of all religions too.

Worship

For many traditions worship is a daily experience – such as *puja* for Hindus; for others, it is a regular experience, involving gathering with others from the faith tradition to join together – singing, reading, praying, listening, dancing, reciting.

Vocation

For some people, responding to God is a matter of what they do, in terms of a job or career, in their life. Some traditions have monastic callings – when people dedicate themselves entirely to God, and are involved in a life of service and ministry.

Pilgrimage

Many traditions have places of special significance, and believers make special journeys to them – sometimes alone, sometimes with groups.

Changing lifestyle

All religions have 'rules' or expectations about the way to live one's life.

Service and Commitment

Serving others may be a requirement of lifestyle. Many religious traditions encourage their members to see all that they do as a service, or a response to God and those he has placed in their care.

For many, one of the greatest responses to God is the commitment made by believers – they are prepared to give everything: time, money, experience, even life itself – to God.

Retreat or study

Sometimes, people feel the need to get away from the distractions of life that have a negative impact on religious faith and practice. So many traditions try to help believers by offering places and times of retreat so as to concentrate fully on worship, prayer, studying the sacred texts, or sharing faith with others.

Acts of kindness

Almost all religions commend acts of kindness to others, whether or not they are members of the faith community. Some religions expect people to pay a *tithe* (a tenth of one's income), or other annual welfare due.

Check it out

AWE

A sense of fear, and at the same time reverence

Completely overwhelmed by a sense of God's presence

So struck by the beauty of something that you are left almost breathless and speechless

So filled with amazement or wonder that you feel humble and insignificant

Check it out

REVELATION

Something shown or explained that was previously hidden

Something which (or someone who) enables others to learn more, or see something for themselves, about God, life, or eternity

Taking away whatever hides knowledge and understanding about something

Exam Tip

It is very important to select the important points when writing an answer. Try and identify the key word/s in the question, and give specific and relevant information.

Q *State **one** thing Christians believe about life which can help them face its difficulties. [2]*

Look at the columns of bullet points below. Select those that you think would be appropriate as an answer to the above question. Explain why the ones you haven't selected are inappropriate.

- God created the earth.
- All life belongs to God, who is in control.
- God gives people free will, so suffering and unhappiness result from a rejecting of God's ways.
- Life is endurable, and is not a trial; God gives strength to those who believe.
- A person's life is holy and sacred.
- Each individual is unique.
- With every temptation or difficulty, God gives a pathway of escape or success.
- After death is judgement, and those who do wrong will be punished.
- Prayer and worship often give inspiration and strength.
- God is loving and forgiving; and knows everything we have to go through.

Now select one of the other religions you are studying, and write a full answer to the same question from the point of view of that tradition.

God isn't just for Christmas!

Task

- What do you think is meant by the cartoon above?

- Explain **three** ways people could show they believe in God throughout the year.
  Now try and answer the question below. (Use the WAWOS framework! see page 14)

Q *'The only true response to God, or the Ultimate being, is to offer worship and praise.' Do you agree? Give reasons or evidence for your answer, showing that you have thought about more than one point of view* [6]

Whose life is it anyway?

As all religions believe that God or a Supreme Being gave life, so they also believe in the **sanctity of life**.

So, much thought has to be given concerning life and death issues.

However, there is also another belief that influences people's responses and that is **free will**. All religions believe humans were created with the freedom to choose whether to believe in or worship God. They are not puppets, controlled by someone else.

So it is believed people are able to recognise the difference between good and bad. They can also choose how to behave. This is one of the major differences between humans and animals. It also means that humans have huge responsibilities as they have to make choices throughout their lives, and sometimes life and death decisions.

> **SANCTITY OF LIFE** – the belief that all life is sacred and unique.

> **FREE WILL** – the belief that humans are free to choose how to live and behave, and that they are not the same as animals.

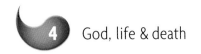

Euthanasia

The word comes from two Greek words meaning 'gentle death' or 'good death'. It is often referred to as 'mercy killing' and means bringing a peaceful end to the dying process. Different terms are used:

Voluntary Euthanasia Actively helping someone to die when they have asked for this to avoid any more suffering.	**'Passive' Euthanasia** When any form of treatment allowing a person to be kept alive is withdrawn, e.g. a life-support machine is switched off. This may be particularly the case when someone is considered brain dead.	**Compulsory Euthanasia** Ending the life of someone who has not asked for it. This has been done during times of 'ethnic cleansing', such as in Nazi Germany, when old, disabled, or people declared of lower racial status, were put to death.
asked for	ending life-support	not asked for

There are also important issues to consider when thinking about euthanasia:

- The final stage of life is important to the individual, the family and others (although many would see it as acceptable to control or ease pain).
- The hospice movement, with the care of the dying and their families, is preferred by many as an alternative.
- Allowing death to occur, or switching off a life support machine when there is no possibility of independent life is not the same as deliberately causing death.
- It is not always appropriate to prolong life at all costs – non-treatment is an option in some circumstances, and this is not the same as deliberately taking a life.

Mother to die after 21 years in coma

A MOTHER who has been in a coma for more than 21 years since giving birth to a son she has never known will finally be allowed to die after a ruling in the High Court today.

Doctors at an unnamed London hospital were given the go-ahead to switch off life support machines after her husband and son agreed the time was right to let her die.

Senior Family Division judge Mr Justice Johnson granted the NHS Trust a declaration allowing it to stop keeping the 54-year-old woman alive.

(*The Evening Standard*)

Task

- Look at the stimulus on the left, and answer the following questions.
  - (a) What kind of euthanasia is referred to in the newspaper article? [2]
  - (b) What might
    - (i) doctors need to consider before making their decision? [4]
    - (ii) the family need to consider before making their decision? [4]
  - (c) 'It is cruel to keep someone alive on a machine when they have been in a coma for ten years.' Do you agree? Give reasons or evidence to support your answer, showing that you have considered more than one point of view. [6]

Suicide

This is the word for taking one's own life intentionally. Most suicides happen because of despair or desperation. Most people think that there is something wrong in a society where people feel suicide is their only option. The Samaritans are an organisation which offers help to anyone contemplating suidice.

A Reference Point!

When faced with a moral dilemma, believers often want to look to sacred texts and try to interpret them for the situation and their life today. Two such issues would be:

● euthanasia

● suicide

A depressed person has a million different things they want to say. But instead of just saying them they tend to bottle them up inside. You might be able to help. Talk to them, try and find out what's bothering them. Maybe even suggest a phone call to the Samaritans.

The Samaritans
Whatever you're going through we'll go through it with you.
08457 90 90 90

Christianity ✟

Christians believe that not only is life sacred, but that God is interested and involved in a person's life too. Therefore, it is possible to take personal problems and difficulties to God, and ask for strength and guidance to deal and cope with them.

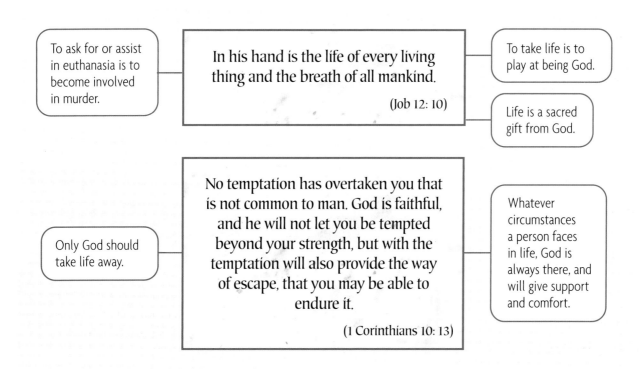

To ask for or assist in euthanasia is to become involved in murder.

In his hand is the life of every living thing and the breath of all mankind.

(Job 12: 10)

To take life is to play at being God.

Life is a sacred gift from God.

Only God should take life away.

No temptation has overtaken you that is not common to man. God is faithful, and he will not let you be tempted beyond your strength, but with the temptation will also provide the way of escape, that you may be able to endure it.

(1 Corinthians 10: 13)

Whatever circumstances a person faces in life, God is always there, and will give support and comfort.

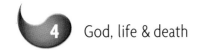

Hinduism

Hindus believe everything living and growing is interconnected. Life is sacred and worthy of the highest respect.

Hindus and Euthanasia

As life is given by a Supreme Being, it's up to him when a life should end. Respect and support should be given to those who are ill. It is believed that each individual has a right time when they will die. To help someone commit suicide would bring bad *karma*.

> The one who tries to escape from the trials of life by committing suicide will suffer even more in the next life.
>
> (Yajur Veda 40–43)

Hindus and Suicide

Suicide is generally against teachings; a person should concentrate on life's goals instead. There is a concept of 'willed death' when a person is ready to give up the earthly world and become a *sanyasin*. There are some Hindus who would say that suicide can be acceptable when carried out as a sacrificial or religious act.

Islam ☪

Muslims believe that every soul was created by Allah. For those who are undergoing mental or physical pain then they need to remember that what happens in this life is a test for the Day of Judgement. The Prophet Muhammad said that anyone who commits suicide will not be shown mercy on the Day of Judgement.

The *Shariah* lists conditions under which life may be taken – but euthanasia is not included.

> Do not kill anyone whom Allah has forbidden you to kill, except for a just cause. If anyone is killed unjustly, we have given his heir authority, but let him not carry his revenge too far; he will be helped.
>
> (Surah 17: 33)

Allah has a plan for each life.

> No one dies unless Allah permits. The term of every life is fixed.
>
> (Surah 3: 145)

As Allah created each soul, so no one has the right to take their own or anyone else's life.

Judaism

Killing in self-defence is allowable, but rarely will euthanasia be committed in such circumstances. However, there is an understanding that suicide, when performed as a sacrificial or religious act, is acceptable. Although there is the belief in God as the Creator, people were also given free will.

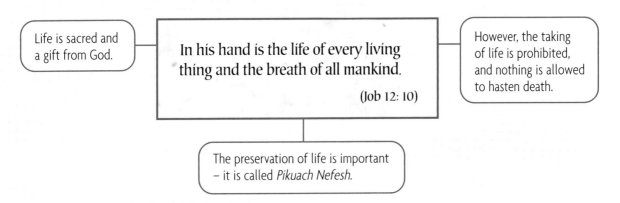

Life is sacred and a gift from God.

In his hand is the life of every living thing and the breath of all mankind.

(Job 12: 10)

However, the taking of life is prohibited, and nothing is allowed to hasten death.

The preservation of life is important – it is called *Pikuach Nefesh*.

Exam Tip

When a question quotes a specified text think carefully about the meaning of the text. If you refer to a text in your answer check that it is really about the question being asked!

Q *'In his hand is the life of every living thing and the breath of all mankind.' (Job 12:15) How might this passage be interpreted by Christians or Jews when thinking about euthanasia?* [4]

Look at the answer below. It has misused the quotation, and failed to answer the question being asked here. Write a more accurate answer. Then find a suitable quotation and write an answer from the other religious tradition you are studying.

Task

- After you have read pages 84–88, using the format for 'Check it Out', decide on four definitions of the key concept *After Life*. Remember to include a symbol.

Answer

The passage in Job 12 makes it clear that every living thing belongs to God – he created them all, out of nothing, and breathed their breath into them. That means that he owns them and is 'in charge of them' as it were. So it is not up to others to decide what happens This is what Christians believe.

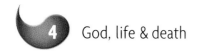

Is that it?

Death is a fact of life: everyone must die at some time. Religions all have teachings about what happens at death and after it. They also have ceremonies or rituals to mark the passing away of the deceased.

Christianity ✠

Christians believe that death is not the end, nor need it be seen as a great tragedy – for they believe that there is an eternal life after death for believers. They believe that to face death as a Christian is to have a certain and sure hope: *'Even if I walk through the dark valley of death, I will not be afraid, because you are with me.'* [Psalm 23: 4]

Eternal life is received through faith. Although bodies grow old and die, Christians believe there is a life after with Christ in heaven: *'We Believe in the resurrection of the body and the life everlasting.'* [The Apostles' Creed]

Timing of an individual's death is in God's hands: *'In his hand is the life of every living thing and the breath of all mankind.'* [Job 12: 10]

Entry to heaven is dependent on two things:

- how a person responds to Jesus and his teachings: *'For God loved the world so much that he gave his only son so that whoever believes in him may not be lost but have eternal life.'* [John 3: 16]

- the way a person responds to those in need on earth: *'I tell you the truth. Anything you did for any of my people here, you also did it for me ... Come and receive the kingdom prepared for you ...'* [Matthew 25: 34, 40]

Jesus also described heaven as a party, a banquet to be enjoyed (Luke 14: 15-24).

Resurrection is the main theme of Christian funeral services – in fact the service usually starts with Jesus' words from John 11: *'I am the resurrection and the life ...'* Ministers or priests may also wear white, a traditional symbol of life after death and resurrection. The resurrection of the dead is a central belief in Christianity – because of the resurrection of Jesus. Belief in life after death is also important for the Christian idea of justice.

New earth and heaven will be made after the judgement day. Sin, death and evil will be finally destroyed forever, and Christians believe that the resurrection of Jesus was a victory over death and sin that all believers can share for themselves. So Christians believe that, in a sense, heaven is already present in believers through Jesus' resurrection.

After-life is a spiritual existence. Those 'redeemed' through Jesus will be resurrected to this new life in the new earth and heaven. There they will worship God and enjoy his presence, and live without sorrow or pain: *'God will wipe away every tear from their eyes. There will be no more death, sadness, crying or pain. All the old ways are gone.'* [Revelation 21: 4]

Life choices are therefore very important. Christians see hell – the opposite of heaven – as a state of being separated from God through one's own deliberate rejecting of God and his ways whilst on earth.

Living a life of love towards others is the way to receive the gift of eternal life from God. Christians believe that there will be a judgement; a time when Jesus will return to earth again, and separate people into two groups – those who have behaved in a loving way towards others, and those who have not. The former receive eternal life, and the latter, eternal punishment.

Interment (burial in the ground) is a choice some Christians prefer, although many will be cremated. For those buried, a cross or memorial stone may be placed at the place of burial (cemetery), and some Christians will visit the grave on the anniversary of death. For those cremated, the ashes may be scattered. In some burials, the coffin will be sprinkled with holy water, and the priest will say: 'In the waters of baptism *N* died with Christ and rose with him to new life. May *he/she* now share with him eternal glory.'

Funeral services may include a *Eucharist* (Communion, or Mass); Many Roman Catholic funerals have a Requiem Mass. At funerals, after the opening words from John 11, or a similar passage from the Bible, there will be some readings, and the singing of a hymn or two. The minister, or person leading the service, will say a few words about the dead person's life, and how they will be missed, and remind the family and friends of the importance of the resurrection and the new life that comes.

Ending the burial service will usually be the words of committal: 'Earth to earth, ashes to ashes, dust to dust: in sure and certain hope of the resurrection and eternal life through our Lord Jesus Christ, who died, was buried and rose again for us. To him be glory forever and ever.' A service of cremation may have slightly different words, but the meaning will be much the same. Usually there will be refreshments for family and friends afterwards, where guests will share in their sorrows, and also their memories and beliefs.

As the embodied soul
continually passes,
in this body, from
childhood to youth,
and then to old age,
the soul similarly
passes into another
body at death.
The self-realised soul
is not bewildered by
such a change.

(Bhagavad Gita 2: 13)

Hinduism ॐ

Hindus believe that for the majority of people this is not their first life, but their soul has been reincarnated from a previous body. Death is considered as a doorway to the next birth.

Retirement (*vanaprastha*) or renunciation (*sannyasa*) stages in life are expected to help Hindus prepare for death. During these stages Hindus may concentrate on spending more time with their family, doing charity work, going on pilgrimages or renouncing worldly possessions and ties.

Euthanasia and artificial extensions of life are disapproved of – there should be a natural end.

Immediate family will normally carry out any rituals needed once the death has happened. This includes preparing the body by putting water from the River Ganges or a tulsi leaf into the mouth. The *antyyesti* (death rituals) allow the family to say goodbye and express their emotions.

Next day the funeral should take place. The ceremony is usually led by the priest and the eldest son.

Cremation is always preferred as it helps to release the *atman* (soul). Hindus consider their life as a sacrifice and this is the final sacrifice. Only *sadhus* (holy men) and children may be buried.

Ashes should be scattered in running water. Many Hindus try to take the ashes to spread on the River Ganges.

Rituals help bring peace to the departed soul. The first *shraddha* (paying respect to one's ancestors) includes a symbolic offering of water and rice cakes.

Near relatives collect for a reading of scriptures which stress that death is the door which must be passed through from birth to birth. *'Only the material body of the indestructible, immeasurable and eternal living entity is subject to destruction; therefore fight, O descendent of Bharata' (Bhagavad Gita 2: 18)*

Annual commemorations are held to remember the deceased.

Transmigration or reincarnation is the term often used for the atman leaving one body and entering another. It is believed to take place over and over again from one species to another depending upon a person's *karma*.

Eventually it is hoped that by living pure lives this cycle of repeated births will stop and the soul will be reunited with God by attaining *moksha* (salvation).

Islam ☪

The Qur'an includes many teachings about *akhirah* or life after death. Muslims believe all that they do on earth will be judged and used in evidence on the Day of Judgement.

Allah knows the time of a person's birth and death long before they are born: '*No one dies unless Allah permits. The term of every life is fixed.*' (Surah 3:145)

Kindness is shown by sitting next to someone dying, to read from the Qur'an and help them recite the *Shahadah* – the declaration of faith. The dying person should lie facing Makkah. The *adhan* (call to prayer) should be the final words heard – just as they were the first. The body should be washed and prepared for the funeral.

Hajji (men who have been on hajj) will have the *ihram* (robe) they wore on pilgrimage draped over them.

Imam leads the prayers in the Mosque and at the graveside. The funeral should take place within 24 hours after the death. Usually only men attend. The body is buried as Muslims believe the body should be placed in contact with the earth. The ceremony should be as simple as possible. Expensive memorials should not be set up.

Releasing of the soul happens straight after death. It is taken by the Angel of Death to a state of waiting until the Day of Judgement.

Angels will have recorded a person's deeds during their life-time. This will include what they have believed, and how they have lived. This evidence will be used on the Day of Judgement. The righteous will go to Paradise and the unrighteous to Hell.

Hell and Paradise are described in the Qur'an. Paradise is described as a beautiful garden with rivers of milk and honey while Hell is described as a terrifying place of heat and torment. '*Those who believe and do righteous deeds are the best creatures. Their reward is with their Lord – Gardens of Eden, underneath which rivers flow, where they shall dwell for ever. Allah is well pleased with them and they are well pleased with Him. This is for those who fear their Lord.*' (Surah 98: 5–8)

Judaism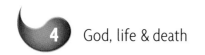

In Judaism it is considered important to focus on what is happening during life rather than being concerned about what may happen in the after-life. *'In his hand is the life of every living thing, and the breath of all mankind.' (Job 12: 10)*

Reform and Orthodox Jews have different views and practices. Most Jews believe in resurrection of the soul, and Orthodox Jews believe in resurrection of the soul **and** the body.

Euthanasia and autopsies are disapproved of. Orthodox Jews believe the body should be returned to God in as natural a condition as possible.

Synagogues will play an important role. If there is no one else then members of the *Chevra Kaddisha* (literally, 'Holy Society') will sit with the dying person. These volunteers will help prepare the body. Sometimes a *tallit* (prayer shawl) with one of the fringes cut will be placed over the body.

Usually the funeral should take place within 24 hours.

Rabbi conducts the service at the cemetery, *Bet Hayyim*. Prayers and Psalms will be read.

Resurrection of the dead is believed in by many Jews. The translation of the Hebrew name for a Jewish cemetery is 'House of Life'.

Everyone present will throw a spadeful of earth into the grave to acknowledge that the body has returned to the earth and the soul waits for resurrection. Later they will wash their hands to symbolise their separation from the dead.

Care of the living is considered important. Close family of the deceased will stay at home for seven days and allow friends to take care of everyday chores. This period of time is called *shiva*, and allows people to withdraw from normal life, and grieve.

Tombstone consecration happens within the next year. At this ceremony the cover over the tombstone is removed, Psalms will be recited and a brief eulogy made. Usually stones are placed on the grave, not flowers.

Immortality of the soul is believed in by most Jews. Progressive Jews believe that only the soul will be resurrected, while Orthodox Jews expect the bodies to be raised as well. Jews believe everyone will be judged and that those who led a good life will be close to God and those who have done wrongs will require purification in Hell.

Observance of the anniversary of the death (*yarzheit*) happens each year. Sons of the family will recite *kaddish*, and a candle symbolising the departed soul burns for 24 hours.

Names of the dead will often be placed upon plaques in synagogues so that the community may remember them.

Exam Tip

When giving an answer about a religion's teachings or practices, be sure to give specific examples. Too many candidates do not describe the content clearly.

Q *Describe the teaching about the after life from **two** religious traditions.* [6]

Look at the two answers below. Neither of them has given a full answer. Can you explain why? Choose one answer, and amend it so that it would gain full marks.

Answer A	Answer B
(i) Name of religious tradition: **Christianity** Teaching: When death comes you can go to hell or heaven depending on whether or not you have been good. If you were in-between you will be sent to hell for a short time to be relieved of 'bad sin'. (ii) Name of religious tradition: **Islam** Teaching: When Muslims die, they believe it is important to bury the body quickly, because there is a judgement after death.	(i) Name of religious tradition: **Hinduism** Teaching: Hindus believe in being born again after death, depending on how you have lived your life. So you have to be good to get a good life; or you might be born again as a dog or cat. (ii) Name of religious tradition: **Christianity** Teaching: Christians believe that there is a life after death – when the person either goes to heaven (where Jesus is), or hell – which is a place of punishment. Your destination is based on the life you lead.

TEST IT OUT

Here is a typical set of examination questions for this unit. Write out answers to them, trying to take account of the Exam Tips and information you have been given.

(a) What is 'awe'? [2]

(b) State **two** ways in which believers might experience 'God'. [2]

(c) Although Christians believe in one God, they also describe God as 'Trinity'. What does this mean? [4]

(d) Why might some religious believers feel that euthanasia is unacceptable? [4]

(e) Describe the teachings on judgement, or what happens at death as a result of one's life according to **two** different religious traditions. [6]

(f) 'People who believe life belongs to God should find that their faith and worship give them the strength to live.' Do you agree? Give reasons or evidence for your answer, showing that you have thought about more than one point of view. [6]

5 Is it fair?

What is fair?

Task

- Make a list of things you think are unfair in *your* life.

'It's not fair!' How often do we hear this said?

But are these things really unfair? Of course it seems so at the time; but not when compared to the situations in other people's lives.

Most people would agree that **fairness** has a lot to do with having the same opportunities and rights as other people, and a sense of being valued and loved for being the people we are.

In the same way, **unfairness** is when those opportunities are taken away or prevented for some reason, and when there is dishonesty, and people are not valued.

Sometimes, there may be good or just reasons why not everyone can have exactly the same as others; but very often what prevents equality are the actions and decisions of people, politicians and governments.

Sometimes fairness and unfairness depends on a person's parents and place of birth.

All religions have understandings about why there is an imbalance in the world, and teachings as to what could and should be done to improve the situation.

Task

• Now make a list of things you think are unfair *in the world*.

Check it out

JUSTICE

- Fairness
- Honest actions
- Freedom from oppression
- Where human rights are observed
- Where everyone has equal provisions and opportunity
- When people treat each other without discrimination or prejudice

Check it out

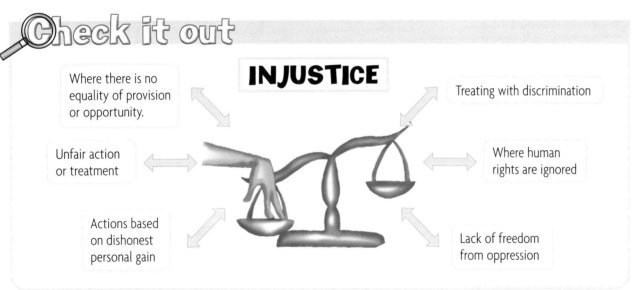

INJUSTICE

- Where there is no equality of provision or opportunity.
- Treating with discrimination
- Unfair action or treatment
- Where human rights are ignored
- Actions based on dishonest personal gain
- Lack of freedom from oppression

All religions try to achieve justice in the world and try to campaign against different types of injustices. Sometimes this has led to conflict with the authority of governments who allow these injustices to happen.

Task

• Create a collage from the media to show justices and injustices. Try to remember some of the examples— they could be useful in evaluative exam questions!

Prayers

One Race the Human Race

'Love one another as sisters and brothers should, and have a profound respect for each other.'

RACIAL JUSTICE SUNDAY 9th SEPTEMBER 2001

Hold Vigils

Fasting

Organise Special Days

We protest

Collections of Money

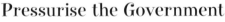
Pressurise the Government

Organise Campaigns

CIVIL DISOBEDIENCE – When people do non-violent actions, such as: refusing to pay taxes; peacefully blocking a roadway; picketing or marching with placards, etc.

Taking part in these sorts of activities means that religious believers are putting pressure on, or challenging those in authority – perhaps government officials, local councils or groups. Sometimes believers are prepared to take part in acts of '**civil disobedience**' and risk being imprisoned or taken before the law courts as a result.

Exam Tip

Use the stimulus provided in the examination paper to help you. **Never** just copy words, phrases, nor simply describe the picture. The stimulus should help you remember things you have studied or discussed. It will give you ideas to write about and either explain or state your own views and ideas.

Task

- Using the page of stimulus opposite entitled 'We Protest', answer the questions, putting into practice the advice in the Exam Tip above.

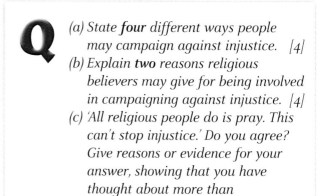

Q (a) State **four** different ways people may campaign against injustice. [4]

(b) Explain **two** reasons religious believers may give for being involved in campaigning against injustice. [4]

(c) 'All religious people do is pray. This can't stop injustice.' Do you agree? Give reasons or evidence for your answer, showing that you have thought about more than **one** point of view. [6]

Check it out

AUTHORITY

People with some 'presence' or character

Right or power over others

The person or group who makes decisions

The moral power behind a person's words or actions

The law or those who ensure it is kept/enforced

Check it out

RESPONSIBILITY

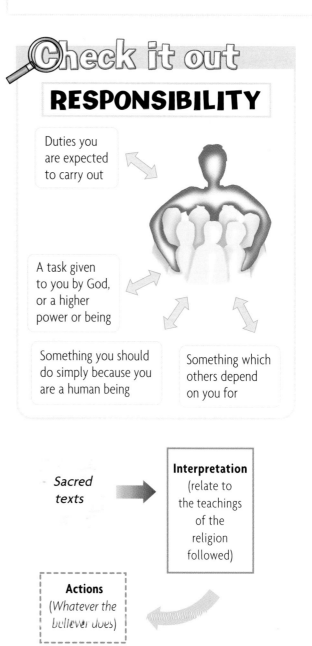

Duties you are expected to carry out

A task given to you by God, or a higher power or being

Something you should do simply because you are a human being

Something which others depend on you for

Sacred texts → **Interpretation** (relate to the teachings of the religion followed)

Actions (Whatever the believer does)

Reference Points!

All religions will encourage believers to speak out against injustice, and to carry out their responsibilities. Believers will decide how to act by interpreting the teachings of their holy books.

Christianity

TEXT

I was hungry and you gave me food, I was thirsty and you gave me drink, I was a stranger and you welcomed me, I was naked and you clothed me, I was sick and you visited me, I was in prison and you came to me. ... And the King will say to you, as you did it to one of the least of these my brethren, you did it to me.

(Matthew 25: 40)

INTERPRETATION

Christians believe that showing concern for others, especially if they are in need, is a basic duty. Jesus taught that and demonstrated it in his own life, and expected his followers to do likewise. So one is not just doing the kind deed for the person who is suffering, but it is as if you are doing it for or to Jesus himself.

Helping others, in whatever way is needed, is a religious duty; failing to do it, is failing God, and failing to live as true human beings.

The ways in which help and support are to be given are both simple and practical, and need not involve money. Kind and thoughtful actions are seen as being of as much value as gifts of money. The reason for helping is as important – if not more so – than the help actually given.

ACTIONS

Many Christians, and some Christian churches or charities, try to give practical help for those in need – such as the following:

- Soup runs
- Night shelters
- Visiting the house-bound
- Counselling offenders
- Building and running hostels

One of the most well known Christian providers of this kind of action is The Salvation Army; but many other Christian churches, and individuals try to follow Jesus' teaching in the verse from Matthew 25.

 **Look it up**

www.salvationarmy.org.uk

TEXT

A new commandment I give to you, that you love one another; even as I have loved you, to you also love one another.

(John 13: 34)

INTERPRETATION

Christians also believe that caring for and sharing with others – in other words 'loving' them – is not only a religious duty, but a command of Jesus himself. Jesus said that only loving the people who love you in return is not difficult; loving someone who is your enemy, or who dislikes you, or someone who is a complete stranger, is another matter. So Christians try to put this into practice in their day to day lives, and also give to support organisations that do it globally.

ACTIONS

Identify: *What is Christian Aid?*
It is a charity organisation working in partnership with local organisations in over 60 countries in the Developing World.

Mention: *Which religion does it belong to?*
Christian. In fact it is supported by more than 40 different Christian denominations in the UK.

Précis: *What are the main aims of the organisation?*

Christian Aid says:

- To expose the scandal of poverty.
- To contribute to the eradication of poverty.
- To challenge systems and processes that marginalise the poor.
- To be inspired by the Gospel of good news to the poor, which promises a fulfilling life for all and the hope of a new earth.

Acknowledge: *What are the main aspects of their work?*

- To improve the lives of people in poor countries.
- To support projects run by partners in the countries.
- To support the poorest groups of people, whatever their religion or culture.
- To campaign for fair trade and greater equality.
- To educate others into the causes of poverty and needs of the poor.

Consider: *How does the work demonstrate the teachings of the religion? Christian Aid says:*
It works on the basis of belief in: a God who loves the world and all who are in it; following the example of Jesus; speaking out against injustice as the prophets did; and the vision of the kingdom of God, which offers life and hope.

Tell: *A specific example of a long or short term project.*
In Senegal, Christian Aid works with local Cooperatives of Farmers – such as the FEGPAB (*) group at Diourbel. Here a number of active projects are funded by Christian Aid and organised by the FEGPAB management group:

- Farming and environment: including reforestation, animal fattening, producing animal feeds, building manure ditches.
- Training: including literacy classes (for women), management classes (budgets, etc.), and a theatre group to communicate ideas visually/dramatically to help the illiterate.
- Village water: well digging (2 per year) and irrigation systems.
- Commercialisation: to prepare for self sufficiency (through co-operative seed banks)
- Savings and credits: giving access to money through loans at low interest to allow trading and development.

(* FEGPAB is from the French for 'Baol Federation of Peasant Groups of Agricultural Workers'.)

See page 25 for IMPACT formula

Look it up

www.christian-aid.org.uk

There are other similar charities:
www.cafod.org.uk   www.tearfund.org.uk

TEXT

And he made from one every nation of people to live on all the face of the earth, having determined allotted periods and the boundaries of their habitation.

(Acts 17: 26)

There is neither Jew nor Greek, there is neither slave nor free, there is neither male nor female; for you are all one in Christ Jesus.

(Galatians 3: 28)

INTERPRETATION

Christians believe that God is the creator of all people and nations, so everyone is equal. They also believe that humans are 'made in the image of God', and so have infinite value. As such, there should be no distinctions or advantages: all people should be treated equally as a 'child of God', and all should share with each other the good gifts God has provided in the world.

Jesus himself showed in his teaching and in his example, that every individual is of value and importance.

Christians have generally spoken out against prejudices based on race, gender, wealth or condition.

ACTIONS

Impact: *What is Catholic Association for Racial Justice (CARJ)?*
It is a charity which works to encourage racial justice.

Mention: *Which religion does it belong to?*
It is a Christian charity, from the Roman Catholic denomination.

Précis: *What is the main aim of the organisation?*
- To raise awareness of the importance of racial justice.
- To understand human feelings of people from different different cultures.
- To develop the theology of being 'One in Christ'.
- To tackle issues of structural injustice.

Acknowledge: *What are the main aspects of its work?*
- Education and publications – to raise awareness and provoke challenge and thought.
- Advocacy – to offer help to individuals suffering harassment.
- Holding regional conferences and group sessions.
- Actively supporting Racial Justice Sunday (2nd Sunday of September) and the promotion of spiritual growth and development.
- Raise awareness and offer support to refugees and asylum seekers.

Consider: *How does the work demonstrate the teachings of the religion?*
The work demonstrates the belief that all people are 'One in Christ' (Gal 3: 28) and the call to 'Love each other like brothers and sisters' (Romans 12: 10). The organisation encourages Christians to: (1) Pray – and engage with the hard issues of racial justice; (2) Think through racial justice issues; (3) Take action that truly makes a difference; (4) Raise funds for local and national initiatives.

Tell: *an example of a long or short term project.*
CARJ has raised an awareness of the needs of refugees and asylum seekers entering into the UK.

Branches have responded in different ways. E.g. in Cardiff Archdiocese, some schools held a Racial Justice Week with the chosen theme of 'Refugees'. Speakers came from a variety of organisations, and schools held liturgies, and produced booklets written by pupils. In Nottingham, members joined local council groups to befriend refugees, provide items of clothing, circulate press statements condemning the inflammatory language of politicians, and took part in Radio interviews. A factsheet was distributed focusing on myths and misinformation about refugees.

CARJ also works with other organisations in promoting Racial Justice Sunday (e.g. Evangelical Christians for Racial Justice (ECRJ); Christians for Racial Justice (CRJ); and the Churches Commission for Racial Justice (CCRJ).

 **Look it up** www.carj.co.uk

Hinduism

TEXT

Perform your prescribed duty which is better than not working. Whoever does not work will not succeed even in keeping his body in good repair.

(Bhagavad Gita 3: 18)

INTERPRETATION

Hinduism teaches that all people are spiritually equal, but that there are different duties in life (*dharma*) that people need to fulfil and accept as they are a result of actions in a previous life (*karma*). The dharma or duties will depend upon the *varnas* or divisions they are born into. Some Hindus believe each person belongs to the same varna for the whole of their lives. Within each varna there are smaller groups called *jatis*. In addition to the four varnas there is a fifth group, which today are called *dalits* (oppressed). They used to be known as 'untouchables', and were considered to be unclean. They had to live in poor conditions and were not allowed to worship in the temples or use village wells.

ACTIONS

Gandhi spoke out against untouchability and renamed them 'Harijans' (Children of God). In 1948 a law was passed to abolish untouchability.

He said: *'I would far rather that Hinduism died than untouchability lived.'*

There are **four** main *varnas*:
Brahmins (priests)
Kshatnyas (warriors)
Vaishyas (trade and skilled workers)
Shudras (unskilled workers)
Each *varna* is subdivided into *Jatis*.
The *harijans* or *dalits* are often referred to as 'outcastes'.

Many dalits live in poor conditions

TEXT

The gods have not ordained hunger
to be our death: even to the well-fed
death comes in various shapes.
The riches of those who are generous
never waste away, while those who will
not give find none to comfort them

(Rig Veda 10: 117)

INTERPRETATION

Like all other possessions Hindus believe wealth is temporary and that attachment to worldly goods (materialism) can hinder people attaining *moksha* (liberation from the cycle of birth and death). Hindus believe they are not the owners of wealth but trustees of what God has lent them. While they are on this earth it is important to help others. One of the four aims in life for Hindus is *artha* – to make wealth to support others.

Feeding the Hungry Worldwide

ACTIONS

Identify: *What is Food for Life?*
It is a charity project working in over 60 countries in the world and distributes free vegetarian food. It is the largest vegetarian/vegan food relief in the world.

Mention: *Which religion does it belong to?*
The International Society of Krishna Consciousness (ISKCON) – a branch of Hinduism – started and supports the Food for Life charity.

Précis: *What is the main aim of the organisation?*
To provide vegetarian food and support to those in need.

Acknowledge: *What are the main aspects of their work?*
To provide free vegetarian meals, companionship and advice to those in need. There are many centres throughout the world. Over 400 free meals are provided each day to the homeless in London.

Consider: *How does the work demonstrate the teachings of the religion?*
The project was started by Swami Srila Prabhupada, who asked followers to not allow anyone within 10 miles of the temple to go without food. It only prepares vegetarian food and exemplifies the importance placed on hospitality in the Hindu tradition.

Tell: *A specific example of a long or short term project.*
During the dreadful floods in Mozambique whole villages were covered in water and entire crops destroyed, with land unable to be used for the next three years. The Food for Life Distribution Programme began by cooking and distributing food to the refugee camps.

Mother feeding child in Mozambique refugee camp

Look it up www.ffl.org/html/

Islam

TEXT

What will convey to you what the steep path is? It is to free a slave, or to give food in the day of hunger to an orphan, next of kin, or to some poor wretch in misery.

(Surah 90: 12-16)

INTERPRETATION

Muslims believe that Allah is the Creator of all humankind, and therefore they must take responsibility and care for others. The community of believers (*ummah*) are expected to care for each other. All wealth is a gift from Allah and so it is important that it is used wisely. A Muslim should not hoard money, or charge interest.

Muslims are encouraged to show care and concern for others in voluntary and compulsory action and giving. *Sadaqah* is voluntary charity given out of kindness. The Prophet Muhammad said that every act done to please Allah or make life more pleasant was sadaqah. Islamic Relief and Red Crescent use money collected by sadaqah in international disasters.

ACTIONS

Zakah This is one of the pillars of Islam, and the compulsory payment of money or possessions to help the poor and needy. It is considered an act of worship (*ibadah*). Each year a Muslim will give about 2.5% of savings to support the needs of others. Each Mosque will have a collecting box and a committee to decide how the money should be spent. Through this system the whole ummah is made more equal.

TEXT

Believers, stand up firmly for justice, as witnesses for Allah, even though it be against yourselves, or your parents or relations, whether the person is rich or poor. Allah is closer to him than you are. Do not be led by passion, lest you should swerve from the truth. If you twist or turn from justice, Allah is well aware of what you do.

(Surah 4: 135)

INTERPRETATION

Muslims have always considered it important to speak out against injustices. The Prophet Muhammad spoke out against a range of injustices against animals, the poor and widows. He himself married Khadijah, a woman who had been twice widowed.

ACTIONS

Identify: *What is Muslim Women's Help Line?*
It is a support for girls and women which began in 1989. *'Changing Our Community For The Better – One Woman's Life At A Time.'*

Mention: *Which religion does it belong to?* Islam.

Précis: *What is the main aim of the organisation?*
To provide Islamic counselling, practical help and information. The organisation discourages dependency and aims to give them courage to make their choices and decisions for themselves.

Acknowledge: What are the main aspects of their work?

- Telephone support – some people require information or some a befriender for future support.
- Face to face counselling – some clients with complex problems are referred for individual counselling.
- Consultancy – the organisation can provide speakers to attend meetings.

Consider: How does the work demonstrate the teachings of the religion?
It aims to promote the relationships exemplified by the Prophet Muhammad and his family, and as taught in the Qur'an.

Tell: A specific example of long or short term project.
The telephone answering service can deal with a range of problems throughout the day. All conversations are confidential and for many women they are not able to find the support or information they need from any other agency. Advice is often sought concerning family problems, bullying, depression, loneliness, domestic violence and forced marriage.

Look it up
www.amrnet.demon.co.uk

Judaism

TEXT

He has showed you, O man, what is good. And what does the Lord require of you, but to do justice, and to love kindness, and to walk humbly with your God?

(Micah 6: 8)

INTERPRETATION

To treat people justly is as important in Judaism as it is to seek justice. There has been discrimination against Jews for a long time. This is called anti-semitism. The worst example of this happened under the leadership of Hitler in the 1930s and 1940s. During this time nearly seven million people were murdered. This is known as the *Shoah* (Holocaust). Since that time there have been many memorials to try to make sure such inhumanity will never happen again. Since 2001 there has been a Holocaust Remembrance Day in Britain on January 27th.

ACTIONS

The memorial centre of Yad Vashem in Jerusalem seeks to make sure that similar events could never happen again. It contains exhibitions of photographs, documents and artefacts. The Hall of Names records the millions of victims. There is a memorial to the children who died in the concentration camps. Here too is the Avenue of the Righteous Gentiles, where trees are planted to honour non-Jews who helped Jews during that time.

 Look it up http://fcit.coedu.edu/holocaust/site map/sitemap.htm
www.yad-vashem.org.il

Two of the memorial sculptures at Yad Vashem

TEXT

When a stranger stays with you in your land, you shall not do to him wrong. The stranger who stays with you shall be to you as the native among you, and you shall love him as yourself; for you were strangers in the land of Egypt: I am the Lord your God.

(Leviticus 19: 33_34)

INTERPRETATION

In the Talmud it states that 'Charity is equal in importance to the other commandments combined'. Charity isn't considered as merely giving money or helping someone, it's also considered as seeking for justice. Judaism doesn't just consider this a good thing to do but a – a *mitzvah* (required act or obligation).

The performance of every mitzvah begins with a blessing. Tradition says there is no such blessing before the giving of charity as that would delay helping human beings in need.

ACTIONS

Identify: *What is Tzedek?*
Tzedek is a charity which supports the developing world. It is based in the UK and began in 1990.

Mention: *Which religious tradition does it belong to?*
It is a Jewish charity. '*Tzedekah*' is the Hebrew word for justice.

Précis: *What is the main aim of the organisation?*
It has two main aims:

- To provide direct support to the developing world towards the relief and elimination of poverty regardless of race or religion.
- To educate people, particularly in the Jewish community, as to the causes and effects of poverty, and the Jewish obligation to respond.

Acknowledge: *What are the main aspects of their work?*
Tzedek has a number of programmes working in the poorest parts of the world. It supports the work of many projects in Africa and Asia. Wherever Tzedek programmes are set up, it is considered important to draw upon the knowledge of local people. Recent projects have included equipping pre-schools in a squatter settlement, funding environmental education workshops in Zimbabwe, and construction of schools in India. It has a threefold obligation to help Jews, to support the needy among non-Jews, and to care for the environment we all inhabit.

Consider: *How does the work demonstrate the teachings of the religion?*
The work of Tzedek is guided by and expresses Jewish values, understanding charity to be a form of justice. It follows the principles of Maimonides that 'the highest form of charity is to take a poor man into partnership.' Tzedek seeks to work with some of the world's poorest communities. Gideon Sylvester, rabbi at Radlett Synagogue said: 'Tzedek allows us to breathe the pure air of goodness, giving, morality and ethics.'

Tell: *A specific example of long or short term project.*
An example of a long term project is 'The Families of Children Project' which supports widowed and abandoned women in Bangladesh. As part of the project, Tzedek sponsors the cost of a craft teacher to help the women make a living selling hand-made crafts, It is estimated over 200 women will benefit. Apart from learning a skill they will learn basic numeracy, literacy and hygiene.

Dr Jonnie Cohen with members of Sevalaya's self-help groups. Tzedek funded a programme of organisational development

TZEDEK

JEWISH ACTION FOR A JUST WORLD

A Bring and Buy sale to raise funds

Tzedek is funding the salary of this craft teacher

Another fund-raising idea

Look it up

www.tzedek.org.uk

Exam Tip

Sometimes examination questions in this unit ask for the name and a brief description of the work of an agency. **Always** mention specific things done by the agency – be brief and concise. **Read** the question carefully – there will always be a reason or statement showing what sort of agency or work is being asked for.

> **Q** *Describe the work of a religious individual or organisation which helps the poor and needy.* [4]

Note the clear statement about the type of work given in the question and repeated in the answer. **Always** write about an appropriate example.

Look at the answer below Do you think it is worth full marks? Explain why or why not. Then write an answer to the question for each of the religions you are studying, and write about an individual **and** an organisation. *(Remember the IMPACT framework!)*

Answer
Name of individual or organisation: Tearfund
The work they do for the poor and needy: They have supported people that have nowhere to go, with a supply of blankets, food, water, clothes. They also help set up schools, and are concerned about HIV, and bad water supplies. They are always looking for helpers, and funds to raise. It is an organisation supported by many Christians and churches.

Many Christians individually give money to charities or help people near to where they live. They may also give their support by voluntary work, prayer, or gifts of money.

Look it up

www.christiansaware.co.uk
www.tearfund.org   www.christian-aid.org.uk
www.cafod.org.uk   www.traidcraft.co.uk
www.mayc.org.uk/world_action.php
(This site, of the Methodist Association of Youth Clubs) has a lot of material on wealth, poverty and debt relief.

Why are people prejudiced?

Check it out

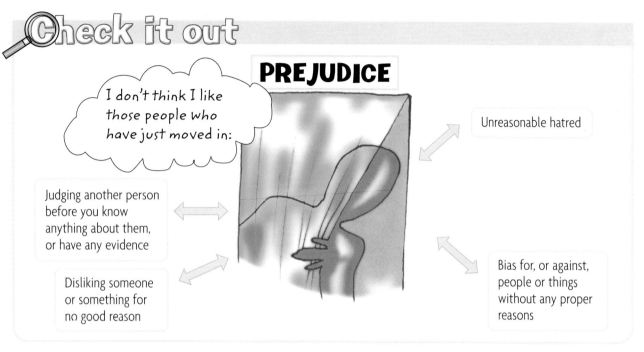

PREJUDICE

I don't think I like those people who have just moved in.

Judging another person before you know anything about them, or have any evidence

Disliking someone or something for no good reason

Unreasonable hatred

Bias for, or against, people or things without any proper reasons

Check it out

DISCRIMINATION

Treating people differently because of race, gender, religion, class, etc

Actions – usually unfavourable – that result from prejudice

Failing to treat people as fellow human beings

To see and respond to people differently because of other factors

Although all religions have clear teachings about prejudice and discrimination, there are many examples of '**institutional racism**' in religions. This shows how difficult it is to ensure that the teachings of a religion are what people put into practice.

INSTITUTIONAL RACISM – Where racist ideas and actions are accepted as common practice, and not condemned

Why do people treat others differently?

PRIDE/SELFISHNESS
Thinking only of self or self-interest; failing to consider the needs of others; jealous of others.

IGNORANCE
Not knowing, or not wanting to know the facts.

EXPERIENCES
Having had an unpleasant experience previously with a particular group of people, or a person from that group.

FEAR
Being uncertain of the implications of others; not sure of the purposes of others; afraid of what might happen.

Reasons for Prejudice

THEOLOGY
Failing to see and believe that all humans are equal in value in their own right.

ANGER/RETALIATION
Reacting after some event or tragedy, thought to be the fault of a particular group of people.

PARENTAL/ PEER PRESSURE
Accepting the views and attitudes of others without questioning or challenging; not thinking for oneself.

Locally, nationally and internationally there are many examples of prejudice and discrimination, despite all the religious teachings against them.

ISLAM

The teachings of Islam include that:

- All people are equal, though not the same.
- All people are important in their own right, as created by Allah.
- We can learn from Muhammad's example (e.g. respect for women).
- The *ummah* (brotherhood) crosses all national, cultural, political, racial and language boundaries.
- The act of prayer stresses the importance of equality. Individuals stand shoulder to shoulder as equal before Allah.

HINDUISM

The teachings of Hinduism include that:

- Each group or individual has its own part to play in life.
- The caste system describes such roles, and need not be discriminatory.
- All human life, whatever caste or 'station' depends on others.
- *Ahimsa* (harmlessness) is a vital aim in life, and discourages discrimination.
- *Karma* (actions) and *dharma* (duty) expect believers to do good and show tolerance.

CHRISTIANITY

The teachings of Christianity include that:

- Prejudice is unacceptable and is against Christian beliefs and teachings.
- God created all human beings as equals, whatever race, ability, or gender.
- The 10 Commandments give guidance on living in harmony with others.
- Jesus' example (e.g. dealing with lepers, outcasts, etc.) and teaching (e.g. Good Samaritan, etc.)

JUDAISM

The teachings of Judaism include that:

- All humanity is made in the image of God.
- All have the same responsibility towards God.
- Being a 'chosen' nation is not being above others, but having additional responsibilities and duties.
- Israel accepts Jews from all nations and races.

RACISM – Discriminating against a person just because of their race or skin colour

Two of the most common examples of people being treated differently are:

- racism
- gender.

GENDER – When discrimination against a person is simply because they are female (or male)

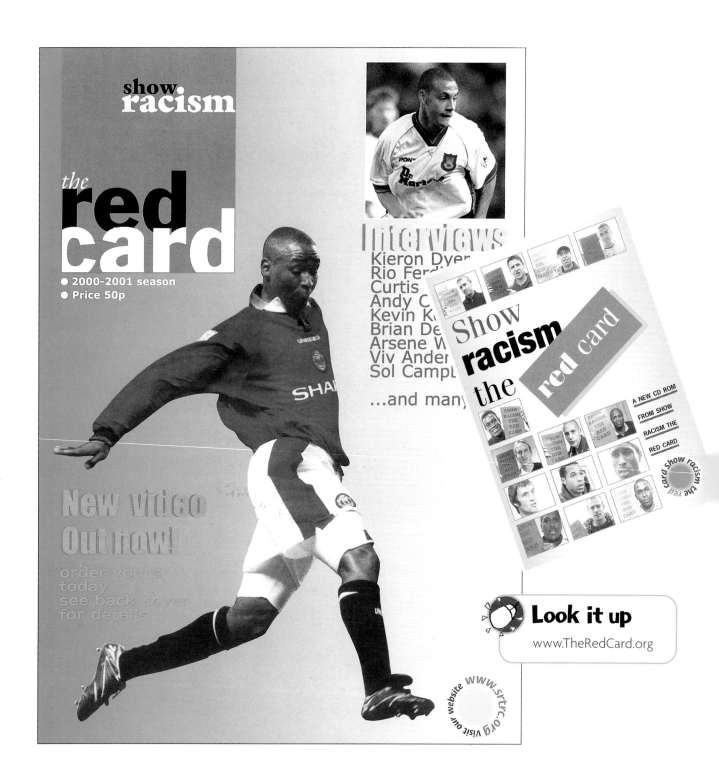

Look it up

www.TheRedCard.org

Although there have been historical interpretations that led to discrimination against women – some still persisting today – religious teachings also highlight the positive role of women in society.

HINDUISM
- It is mainly women who perform *puja* (ceremonial worship) in the home.
- Laws of Manu see women as supported by husbands, or sons, so not needing possessions of their own.
- The Indian Constitution recognises equal rights for men and women.

CHRISTIANITY
- Jesus did not discriminate against women (e.g. John 4: 1–30).
- Men and women are seen to be equal before God (e.g. Gal 3: 28).
- Today in many churches, women are ordained and function as full priests or ministers.

ISLAM
- Men and women are equal before Allah and have the same religious duties and will face the same judgement.
- Women are allowed particular rights and protection (to have no sexual harassment; be cared for in pain or difficult times; to be provided for; to wear the hijab (satr) for keeping modesty.)

JUDAISM
- Women take an important role in religious ceremonies in the home.
- Women have held significant positions in Jewish history.
- Jewish identity is established through the female line.

What do we need and what do we want?

Life under the burden of debt

But Mum, I really need a computer; I can't do half the things I need to do on this old one!

Often people say they 'need' something – when really they mean 'want'. It is very important to separate the two ideas, and most people would agree to the following definitions:

A NEED:
A necessity; something that is a requirement, without which a person would be in poverty or extreme hardship.

A WANT:
A wish or longing for; something that is craved, but which being without would not actually bring hardship.

However, you will find that the words can be used differently.

Task

- Make a list of five things you really do *need* in your life, and five things that you *want* – things you would like to have if you could.

- What do you think would be the list for someone your age living in a country in the developing part of the world?

110

Rights and duties.

In the same way as people easily confuse needs and wants, it is easy to mix up a person's 'rights' and their 'duties', or responsibilities. Many people say that having a right brings with it a duty.

A person's rights

- what a person can expect to have;
- something to which a person is entitled;
- not something earned or deserved;
- something you have by being a human being;
- what the 'law' says you ought to have or be able to do.

A person's duties

- what a person is expected to do;
- something entrusted to you by God or someone in authority;
- something you should do because you are a human being;
- what others are depending on you for.

Attitudes towards and use of wealth resources.

Closely connected to the ideas of 'needs' and 'wants', and also those of 'rights' and 'duties', are questions about wealth and people's attitudes to it, and the way they use whatever resources they have themselves.

Is this 'true' wealth?

I AM AN EXECUTIVE MANAGER, ACTUALLY!

All religions say that material wealth – money, possessions, status – cannot be of lasting value; they are all 'things' that can be lost, stolen, taken away, or can lose their value.

Religious teachings explain the need for careful use of resources, and have a general sense that all that we have is given or loaned to us, or at least that what we do with the resources we have around us will affect others and the quality of their lives.

Where did I put it?

Oh no! It's been stolen!

I thought it was mine?

It is now worthless!

Christianity ✝

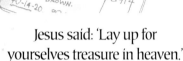

Spiritual values are the most important;

Jesus said: 'Lay up for yourselves treasure in heaven.'

(Matthew 6: 19)

- Material wealth is not the most important thing in life;
- Do not worry or be anxious over money;
- Material wealth should be shared with others;
- True giving, or generosity, needs to involve cost or sacrifice;
- There is no success in relying on money or wealth for security or meaning in life;
- The way you make your money or wealth is just as important as what you do with it.

No unfair methods to get money

No greed or snobbishness

No lending for profit

No gambling

What about the lottery?

Many Christians are very concerned about the National Lottery, and the effect it has on people. They do not think that the 'get rich quick' idea leads to a healthier lifestyle. Many churches have spoken out against gambling, and so feel that the Lottery is unacceptable. Some are also unhappy about receiving lottery money, and are concerned about the number of charities which have suffered through people playing the lottery instead.

A Portrait

World Wide Message Tribe is a Christian pop group, based in Manchester. Andy Hawthorne, the co-founder, gave up an executive job with a large salary so that he could concentrate on the work of WWMT with young people. All seven members of the group deliberately turned their back on wanting to be rich and famous.

'We took a dramatic drop in salary,' says Andy, 'but in terms of fulfilment and satisfaction – there's no comparison. Life doesn't revolve around money; but what I'm doing lasts forever.'

As well as singing and visiting schools, the group also helps fund a special bus as part of the Eden Project, based in Wythenshawe in Manchester. This high tech bus has comfortable seats, videos and electronic games, and enables young people to have a good time, and to talk and think about issues in life and religion. Members of the WWMT, and the Eden Project which it sponsors, believe that quality of life is more important than investment in money, possessions and security.

Hinduism ॐ

Material possessions are not of lasting value:

What's called worldly possessions is impermanent for by things unstable, the stable cannot be obtained.

(Katha Upanishad 2:6, 10)

- Wealth is not owned, it is loaned – by God.
- A person should fulfil their duty through their wealth.
- Personal wealth should be gained through lawful means – *artha*.
- If you are blessed with wealth, be generous and compassionate.

No greed

No bribery

No dishonesty

No illegal means to make money

The gods have not ordained hunger to be our death: even to the well-fed death comes in various shapes. The riches of those who are generous never waste away, while those who will not give find none to comfort them.

(Rig Veda 10: 117)

A Portrait

Remember the Hindu charity Food for Life, referred to earlier?

Look back at the account of its aims and work, and write a description of how it interprets and puts into action Hindu teaching about wealth, and *dana* (charity).

Many Hindus individually give money to charities or help people near to where they live. They may also give their support by voluntary work, prayer, or gifts of money.

Look it up

www.ffl.org/html/

Islam ☪

Proper use of one's wealth is of lasting value:

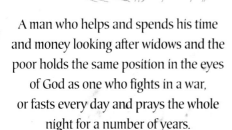

A man who helps and spends his time and money looking after widows and the poor holds the same position in the eyes of God as one who fights in a war, or fasts every day and prays the whole night for a number of years.

(Hadith)

- All wealth is a gift from Allah.
- It is not wrong to be wealthy; the more wealthy you are the more generous you should be.
- Wealth should not be used to harm others.
- Obliged to pay zakah (2.5% of cash wealth).
- Voluntary payments (*sadaqah*) or good actions for charity are encouraged too.

No gambling

No dishonest use of money

No usury (lending for profit)

No dishonest means to get money

 Look it up

www.islamic-relief.com
www.muslimaid.org.uk

A Portrait

Muslim Aid began in 1985. Like many other charities its main aims are to provide help and support to the poorest groups of people, and those suffering disasters. It has projects taking place in over 44 countries in Africa, Asia and Europe. It works through partners in the country it is supporting, and provides emergency relief, as well as clean water, education and health care. Donations of money come from personal donations (sadaqah), from zakat, and from other gifts and legacies.

Many Mulsims individually give money to charities or help people near to where they live. They may also give their support by voluntary work, prayer, or gifts of money.

Muslim Aid WORKING FOR PEOPLE

Judaism

Giving to those in need is a duty:

Don't wear yourself out trying to get rich. Be wise enough to control yourself. Wealth can vanish in the wink of an eye.

(Proverbs 23: 5)

- All possessions belong to God, so should be neither chased after nor rejected.
- A person should budget carefully so as to provide for their family.
- Many families use *pushkes* (collecting boxes); tithing is also encouraged.
- Wealth should be used for the benefit of the community.

No greed

No dishonesty

No selfish use of wealth

No use of money on Shabbat

A Jewish school in London raised funds to equip a pre-school in Zimbabwe.

A Portrait

Remember the work of Tzedek?

Look back at the account of its aims and work (page 102), and write a description of how it interprets and puts into action Jewish teaching about wealth, and charity.

 Look it up

www.tzedek.org.uk
www.jw-relief.co.uk
www.jnf.co.uk

Many Jews individually give money to charities or help people near to where they live. They may also give their support by voluntary work, prayer, or gifts of money.

 Q *Explain what **one** religious tradition teaches about wealth.* [6]

Look at the two answers below. Which of the two do you think is a good and clear answer? Why do you think the other one is not as good?

 Exam Tip

When answering a question that asks for a description of religious teachings, give clear specific points. **Never** write general 'cover-all' comments. Check carefully how many religious traditions you should write about, and write the **correct word** for the religion.

Answer A	Answer B
Name of religious tradition: Islam Teaching about wealth: A Muslim is not allowed to receive interest on their money. Muslims are expected to help the poor by donating at least 2.5% of their earnings to charity. Charity is one of the Five Pillars – zakah. Also your wealth must be gained in an honest work and effort; and gambling is totally unacceptable. The more wealthy a person is, the more generous they can be to those in need.	Name of religious tradition: Christianity Teaching about wealth: You should take as much money as you need and no more. Christians are also expected to be kind and do good, and to help others – whoever they are. A Christian should not be prejudiced against a person of a different race or nationality, and so should help them if they are in need. If they have money to spare then they should be willing to give what they can; as long as they do not harm their own family through it.

Now write your own full answer to the question.

TEST IT OUT

Here is a typical set of examination questions for this unit. Write out answers to them, trying to take account of the Exam Tips and information you have been given.

(a) What is meant by:
    (i) 'justice'
    (ii) 'authority'   [2]

(b) State **two** reasons Christians give for believing all humans beings are equal.   [2]

(c) Explain the difference between people's 'rights' **and** people's 'responsibilities'.   [4]

(d) Give **two** reasons why people may be prejudiced.   [2]

(e) State **two** ways in which people may be discriminated against.   [2]

(f) Explain the teaching about prejudice and discrimination from **two** different religious traditions.   [6]

(g) 'A religious believer has no choice but to fight for racial justice.' Do you agree? Give reasons or evidence for your answer, showing that you have thought about more than one point of view.   [6]

Appendix

Levels of Response Grids for Marking

Level	AO1 and AO2 Descriptors *(for questions about religious teachings and beliefs)*	4 marks	6 marks
1	A relevant statement of information or explanation which is limited in scope or content. OR Makes simple connections between religion and life. Almost no use of specialist language.	1	1
2	An accurate amount of basic information or an appropriate explanation of a central theme or concept. Limited use of specialist language. OR Shows informed awareness of the impact of religion on people's lives. Limited use of specialist language.	2	2
3	An account indicating thorough knowledge and understanding of key ideas or concepts. Where appropriate, some use is made of specialist vocabulary. OR Shows understanding of the relevance or application of religion. Some use is made of specialist vocabulary.	3	3
3	An account indicating thorough knowledge and understanding of key ideas or concepts. Uses and interprets specialist vocabulary in appropriate context. OR Shows understanding of the relevance or application of religion. Uses and interprets a range of religious language and terms in appropriate context.	3	4
4	A coherent account showing awareness and insight into religious facts, ideas and explanations. Clear and accurate use of specialist vocabulary. OR Demonstrates understanding of different ways in which religion has relevance and application. Clear and accurate use of specialist vocabulary.	4	5
4	A coherent account showing awareness and insight into religious facts, ideas and explanations. Specialist vocabulary used extensively and interpreted accurately. OR Competently demonstrates understanding of different ways in which religion has relevance and application. Uses specialist vocabulary extensively and interprets them accurately.	4	6

Level	AO3 Descriptor *(for Evaluative Questions – where you use the WAWOS framework)*	Marks
1	A simple appropriate justification of a point of view.	1
1	And if linked to evidence or suitable example.	2
2	An expanded justification of one viewpoint, with appropriate example and/or illustration. OR A balanced account of alternative viewpoints, with appropriate examples or illustrations.	3
2	An expanded justification, with examples and/or illustration, using relevant evidence and religious or moral reasoning. OR A balanced account of alternative viewpoints with appropriate examples and/or illustrations, using relevant evidence and religious or moral reasoning.	4
3	A thorough discussion of the religious and moral aspects of an issue and their implications for the individual and/or for the rest of society, using relevant evidence and religious or moral reasoning. OR A thorough discussion of the religious and moral aspects of an issue, showing a recognition of some of the complexity of religious issues using relevant evidence and religious or moral reasoning.	5
3	A thorough discussion of the religious and moral aspects of an issue, showing a recognition of some of the complexity of religious issues or their implications for the individual and/or for the rest of society. Makes reasoned judgements based on a range of evidence and well developed arguments.	6

Index

Entries marked in bold refer to key concepts from the specification